JAMES MARTIN'S
GREAT
BRITISH
Adventure

JAMES MARTIN'S
GREAT BRITISH
Adventure

Photography by Peter Cassidy

Hardie Grant
QUADRILLE

Publishing director: Sarah Lavelle
Commissioning editor: Céline Hughes
Project editor: Samantha Stanley
Design manager: Claire Rochford
Photography: Peter Cassidy
Front cover photography: David Venni
Cover hair and make up: Alice Theobold
Cover fashion stylist: Rachel Gold
Text design: Smith & Gilmour
Food preparation and styling:
James Martin and Sam Head
Props stylist: Polly Webb-Wilson
Home economists: Sam Head and Emma Marsden
Production: Tom Moore and Vincent Smith

First published in 2019 by Quadrille Publishing,
an imprint of Hardie Grant Publishing
Quadrille, 52–54 Southwark Street, London SE1 1UN

www.quadrille.com

Text © 2019 James Martin
Photography © 2019 Peter Cassidy
Design and layout © 2019 Quadrille Publishing

Cataloguing in Publication Data: a catalogue record for this book
is available from the British Library.

ISBN: 978 178713 374 7

Printed in China

CONTENTS

INTRODUCTION

Well, where do I even start with writing about the highlights of this trip. Like the French and American books and shows before this one, my Great British Adventure has so much to offer. The country has changed so much over what is a short period of time in terms of its food history. And what a change! The food is so good all over Scotland, Ireland, Wales and England, thanks in part to the amazing people growing, farming, fishing, making, brewing and working in the food and drink industry, making it one of the best in the world.

What is so special is the use of old and new techniques and embracing cultures from around the world that gives us – chefs and cooks – the ingredients to make our job a lot easier. From the tastiest lamb I've ever eaten in the far north of the beautiful Orkney Islands, produced the same way it always has been (from sheep grazed on the seaweed behind the longest man-made sheep dyke on the island of North Ronaldsay) to the best langoustines I've ever eaten, simply cooked and served with mayonnaise on the banks of Strangford Lough in the south-east of Northern Ireland. There's the amazing wine and fizz made by the guys at the Camel Valley Vineyard in Cornwall and the fantastic gin – the best I've ever tasted, by the way – made in small batches at Forager's Gin in Snowdonia in Wales. All of this and so, so much more has helped to put Great Britain firmly on the culinary map of the world.

I've been involved in food all my life, from when I was a young kid helping out at the pig farm back at home. It was there that I got to understand that great food comes from great ingredients. Not just that, though. By working with food, as I do, I feel you have a much better understanding and respect for it. You realise that producing food – either growing, catching or making it – takes a lot of time, skill and hard work, and without a doubt you respect it and the people who produce it so much more.

There are certain things I would love to go back and see again, like the crab fishermen off the coast of Scotland, who brave the seas to bring us the best-tasting crab you will ever eat, to the small batch of pro-foragers who, as I witnessed, brave the rugged Welsh coastline in a tiny canoe to grab some rock samphire and other bits from the overhanging cliffs.

The TV series, of course, only scratched the surface of the amazing things you can find around Britain and I for one didn't want to stop.

The same can be said for the places where we can enjoy eating the food we produce. I don't think there is a country in the world that has managed to change the views that other countries have about their food more than Great Britain, as we found when we had to choose a route around the country. Firstly, I must apologise to the hundreds of food producers and restaurants we didn't get to see and all the counties we had to just drive through – there was little I could do as we had only a few shows to fit it all in.

That said, what treats we found! Starting with the Waterside Inn at Bray, set up by two French brothers who, I think, epitomise the food scene and what's changed over the years. Holding their three Michelin stars for 30 years, the Waterside Inn is a very special place and if it housed a family tree of all the people who have worked there, past and present, you would see how much this place has influenced the industry since it began. There are teams of chefs and waiters in kitchens all over the country who will have had a connection with this place somewhere in their food chain.

Then there are the two best meals I've eaten in this country so far. A big statement, I know, but well worth it. Gareth Ward at Ynyshir is a top-class cook as is Sat Bains, whose restaurant in Nottingham, which sits under a flyover down a pothole-lined road, is one of the best in the world. So much so that I decided to stay after the crew had gone and work the night's service with him and his brilliant team.

But there are so many other people I want to thank for their help on this trip, from Michel Roux Snr to the brilliant writer Grace Dent, who I had a great, fun tour of Birmingham's food scene with. So, there you go – it's really a massive thank you to them all and to all of you for all your support over what is now 25 years on TV. I hope you enjoy the show and, of course, cooking the recipes in this book as much as I've enjoyed making them. Great Britain is a very special place to be and I feel so lucky to live, work and, of course, eat and drink here.

WARNING
RESTRICTED AREA
UNAUTHORISED DIVING
ETC. PROHIBITED

STARTERS & SNACKS

BUFFALO MOZZARELLA, BLACKBERRY & BEETROOT SALAD

It's amazing to think there are thousands of buffalo roaming the British countryside and those at Laverstoke Park Farm in Hampshire, run by Formula One World Champion Jody Scheckter, produce some of the best buffalo mozzarella. This is a fresh cheese that needs to be eaten quickly – it's made by warming and stretching the curd, moulding it into balls and storing it in salted water. This adds flavour but degrades the cheese if kept for too long. (Laverstoke's ice creams are also mega!)

SERVES 2

25ml elderflower cordial
25ml white wine vinegar
50ml olive oil
½ cucumber, deseeded
    and diced
50g blackberries
200g pre-cooked (not pickled
    in vinegar) beetroot, sliced
1 ball buffalo mozzarella
2 pickled onions, halved
    and layers separated

For the curd
500ml buffalo milk
juice of ½ lemon
sea salt and freshly ground
    black pepper

To serve
small handful of bergamot leaves
    or herb flowers (optional)

You will need
a cook's thermometer

Line a sieve with muslin and rest it over a bowl.

To make the curd, pour the buffalo milk into a medium saucepan and place over a very low heat. Heat to 70°C (160°F) – use a cook's thermometer to check – then pour in the lemon juice and whisk well. Spoon into the muslin to strain away the liquid for 2 minutes, then spoon the curd into a separate, clean bowl. Discard the liquid. Season the curd well, mix together and chill.

Whisk the elderflower cordial, vinegar and olive oil together in a bowl, season and add the cucumber and blackberries. Toss together to coat well.

To serve, arrange the beetroot slices on a large serving plate and spoon some of the curd all around. Shred the mozzarella and dot around the plate, then spoon over the dressed cucumber and blackberries, leaving the rest of the dressing in the bowl. Scatter over the onion layers, then spoon over the dressing and decorate with the bergamot leaves or herb flowers, if using.

WILD MUSHROOMS ON TOAST WITH DUCK EGGS & BRITISH TRUFFLE

Cooking with wild mushrooms when they're in season is a real delight. There are over 14,000 types in Britain, though, so it's essential to forage with someone who knows what they're doing. I was in Scotland with Tom Kitchin and we found masses of chicken-of-the-woods and ceps, which he took back to his restaurant in Edinburgh to cook. Truffles are the king of fungi; I've even found some in my local woods. Duck eggs are usually larger then hens', so need a little more cooking. Keeping them in iced water is a great way to enable you to serve several poached eggs at the same time.

SERVES 2

15g butter
300g wild mushrooms
½ garlic clove, crushed
½ shallot, diced
small bunch of flat-leaf
    parsley, chopped
2 slices of sourdough bread
1 tablespoon olive oil
fresh British black truffle,
    to serve (optional)

For the sauce
15g butter
½ garlic clove, crushed
½ shallot, diced
100g wild mushrooms, torn
100ml double cream
sea salt and freshly ground
    black pepper

For the eggs
1 teaspoon white wine vinegar
4 duck eggs

Start by making the sauce. Melt the butter in a small saucepan over a medium heat and sauté the garlic, shallot and torn mushrooms for 2–3 minutes, until just starting to soften. Pour in the cream, season and bring to the boil and simmer for 2–3 minutes. Use a stick blender to whizz the ingredients until smooth to make a sauce, then cover, set aside and keep warm.

Fill a bowl with cold water and ice and put to one side. To poach the eggs, bring a large pan of water to the boil then add the vinegar. Using a whisk, swirl the water around to make a whirlpool in the centre then carefully crack an egg into the centre – you might find it easier to crack it into a ramekin and pour from this. Simmer for 3 minutes then carefully lift the poached egg out using a slotted spoon and gently lower into the bowl of iced water. Cook the remaining eggs and leave them in the iced water. Rinse the pan out, fill with boiling water and keep on a simmer – this is used to reheat the eggs later.

Melt the butter for the mushrooms in a large frying pan over a medium heat. As soon as it's melted, fry the mushrooms with the garlic and shallot for 2–3 minutes. Season well and stir through the parsley.

Toast the sourdough and drizzle with olive oil. Plunge the eggs into the pan of boiling water for around 30 seconds to reheat them, then drain.

To serve, put a piece of toast on each plate, pile the mushrooms over, top each with 2 eggs, spoon over the sauce and grate over the truffle, if using.

CARAMELISED ONION, COURGETTE & WENSLEYDALE QUICHE

'Real men eat quiche' is what the team told me as I made this. I don't know about that, but I can tell you that Wensleydale cheese is a great addition. It was originally made from ewes' milk by French monks from the Roquefort region who settled in Yorkshire, but commercial production by large dairies using cows' milk soon spread throughout Britain. In 2013, Yorkshire Wensleydale was granted PGI (protected geographical indication) status and is now made the proper way in Hawes and is the one to look for.

SERVES 8

1 tbsp olive oil
15g butter
2 red onions, sliced
sea salt and freshly ground
    black pepper
2 eggs
2 egg yolks
300ml double cream
100ml full-fat milk
2 small courgettes, around
    225g, thinly sliced,
    lengthways
3 courgette flowers,
    sliced lengthways
175g crumbled Wensleydale
    cheese

For the pastry
300g plain flour, plus a
    little extra for dusting
150g butter, chilled and diced
a pinch of sea salt
a few thyme sprigs,
    leaves picked (optional)
1 egg, beaten

Start by caramelising the onions for the filling. Heat the oil and butter in a medium pan over a medium heat. Once the butter has melted, stir in the onions and a pinch of salt. Cover and cook over a low heat for 20–25 minutes, stirring every now and then until the onions have softened and caramelised. If they look as though they're burning, add a tablespoon of water and stir in . Spread onto a plate and set aside to cool.

Make the pastry. Put the flour into a bowl, add the butter, salt and thyme (if using) and rub together with your fingertips until the mixture resembles coarse breadcrumbs. Add the egg and mix with a knife until the mixture forms clumps, then bring together lightly with your hands. Add a couple of teaspoons of water if the dough feels dry. Dust a clean work surface with flour and knead lightly and quickly until smooth. Wrap in clingfilm and chill for 30 minutes.

Preheat the oven to 180°C (160°C fan)/350°F/gas 4.

Lightly flour your work surface and roll out the pastry to a rough circle measuring about 32cm in diameter. Carefully lift the pastry into a 27-cm fluted tart tin and gently press into the corners.

To make the filling, put the eggs and egg yolks, cream and milk into a jug and whisk together. Season well and whisk again. Spread the onions over the base of the pastry, arrange the courgettes and courgette flowers on top (see overleaf) and scatter over the cheese. Pour the egg mixture into the tart tin and give it a little shake so that it spreads evenly. Carefully slide the tart tin onto a baking sheet and bake in the preheated oven for 45–50 minutes, until the filling is set.

Once cooked, take the quiche out of the oven, let it sit for about 5 minutes, then trim the pastry edges. Serve hot, warm or cold with a green salad. Leftovers keep very well for the next day but the filling will be a little firmer after a night in the fridge. (Pictured overleaf.)

ONION & STOUT SOUP WITH HOMEMADE BUTTER & SODA BREAD

I love this soup. It's so simple to make and the result you get from just a few ingredients is amazing. Stout, of course, is the key, giving it a real depth of flavour, but make sure you cook the onions until golden brown to get more flavour, too. Soda bread is a great one to start with on your bread-making journey as it's so easy.

SERVES 4

2 tablespoons olive oil
3 medium onions, sliced
250ml stout
500ml beef stock
sea salt and freshly ground
    black pepper
300ml double cream
200g Irish cheddar cheese

For the soda bread
170g self-raising flour
170g plain flour, plus extra
    for dusting
½ teaspoon sea salt
½ teaspoon bicarbonate
    of soda
300ml buttermilk

For the homemade butter
750ml double cream
pinch of sea salt

To serve
25ml double cream
25ml olive oil
50g Irish cheddar
    cheese, crumbled

Preheat the oven to 200°C (180°C fan)/400°F/gas 6.

Heat the olive oil in a large saucepan and stir in the onions. Cook over a low to medium heat for 10–12 minutes until the onions start to soften and turn golden. Pour in the stout and stock, then season and stir everything together. Cover and bring to the boil, then reduce the heat to a simmer and cook for 10–15 minutes.

To make the soda bread, sift both types of flour, the salt and bicarbonate of soda into a large bowl. Make a well in the centre and pour in the buttermilk. Use a round-bladed table knife to mix everything together to make a rough dough, taking care not to overwork it or the finished bread won't be as light.

Divide the dough in half and lift onto a clean work surface and shape each one into a round about 15cm in diameter and 3cm thick. Dust with a little flour and cut a cross on top using a sharp knife. Transfer to a baking sheet and bake for 15–20 minutes until golden. To check the bread is baked all the way through, tap each base – they should sound hollow. If not quite there, return to the oven to continue baking and check after 5 minutes.

To make the butter, put the double cream into the bowl of a freestanding mixer fitted with the whisk attachment and whisk on high speed until the cream separates. Strain the mixture through a sieve lined with muslin into a bowl and lift the solids left in the muslin into a clean tea towel. Wrap the tea towel around them and squeeze out the liquid. (This liquid is buttermilk; you could use it to make more soda bread.) Unwrap the tea towel and place the butter onto greaseproof paper. Sprinkle with a little salt, mix together and shape the butter into a log.

Pour the cream into the soup, then crumble the cheese in. Season and blitz with a stick blender or transfer to a liquidiser and blitz until smooth. Reheat the soup in the pan until heated through.

Ladle the soup into bowls, drizzle with cream and oil, then scatter over the cheese. Serve with the soda bread and homemade butter.

ISLE OF WIGHT DOUBLE-BAKED CHEESE SOUFFLÉS

I used to drive past Briddlesford Lodge Farm on my trips to the Isle of Wight but it's become my first stop when I arrive on the island. The milk from their Guernsey cow herd produces the most fantastic cheese, cream and butter. You can also buy amazing veal from the butcher's shop on site and they make a mean breakfast in the café! Any cheddar cheese will do for this recipe, though, so give it a try.

SERVES 4

40g butter, plus extra,
    softened, to grease
40g plain flour,
    plus extra to dust
250ml milk
200g grated cheddar cheese
1 tablespoon Dijon mustard
1 teaspoon chopped rosemary
sea salt and freshly ground
    black pepper
1 egg yolk
3 egg whites
400ml double cream
small bunch of watercress
1 chicory bulb, chopped
2 little gem lettuce, chopped

For the dressing
1 egg yolk
25ml white wine vinegar
100ml vegetable oil

You will need
4 x 8-cm soufflé moulds/ramekins

Preheat the oven to 200°C (180°C fan)/400°F/gas 6.

Grease the soufflé moulds with butter and dust the insides with flour, tipping out any excess.

Melt the butter in a medium saucepan over a medium heat and whisk in the flour, cooking for about 1 minute. Slowly pour in the milk, whisking all the time, and cook for about 2 minutes. Beat in a third of the cheese and all the mustard and rosemary, then season well, pour into a bowl and leave to cool. Stir in the egg yolk when the sauce has cooled.

Whisk the egg whites in a clean, grease-free bowl until stiff peaks form. Fold into the sauce, then fold in half of the remaining cheese. Spoon evenly into the prepared moulds, then level off the tops. Run your finger around the edge of each soufflé to create a sort-of hat effect. Sit the moulds in a deep roasting tin lined with kitchen paper (to stop the bottoms of the soufflés from catching) and pour water into the tin to about two-thirds of the way up the sides. Carefully transfer to the oven and bake for 12–14 minutes. Remove from the oven and lower the temperature to 180°C (160°C fan)/350°F/gas 4.

Lift each mould out of the roasting tin and run a knife around the edge of the soufflés and turn them out into an ovenproof dish. Allow to cool slightly then pour over the cream and scatter over the remaining cheddar. Return to the oven for 10–12 minutes.

To make the dressing, whisk the egg yolk, vinegar and oil together in a bowl. Season and add a tablespoon of cold water and whisk again to combine.

Put the watercress, chicory and little gem leaves into a bowl and dress with 2 tablespoons of the dressing. (Pour the rest into a clean, airtight jar, store in the fridge and use within a week.) Toss well.

Spoon a soufflé and some sauce onto each plate and serve the salad on the side. (Pictured overleaf.)

DEEP-FRIED SOFT-BOILED EGG SALAD WITH CROUTONS & BACON

I love this salad but you need to serve it on a platter to get the full effect. Use the best eggs and bacon you can afford to get the full flavours; eggs with deep-coloured yolks look great. Don't overcook the eggs, though – 6 minutes should be fine – as you need the yolks to be slightly runny to mingle with the dressing.

SERVES 4–6

12 slices of streaky bacon
½ loaf of sourdough,
    chopped into chunks
6 eggs, unshelled,
    plus 2 eggs, beaten
100g plain flour
sea salt and freshly ground
    black pepper
100g panko breadcrumbs
1–2 litres vegetable oil, for
    deep-frying
125-g bag of salad leaves
2 chicory bulbs, trimmed
    and separated into leaves
1 bunch or 100-g bag of
    watercress
handful of beetroot leaves
2 little gem lettuce, trimmed
    and separated into leaves
6 leafy celery tops

For the dressing
1 tablespoon honey
1 tablespoon Dijon mustard
150ml vegetable oil
50ml white wine vinegar
1 tablespoon grainy mustard

Heat a non-stick frying pan over a medium heat until hot then add the bacon to the pan and fry, turning every now and then, until crisp. Lift onto a plate and set aside. Return the pan to the hob and fry the sourdough chunks in the fat, again over a medium heat, until golden and crisp. Spoon onto the plate with the bacon and set the pan aside to use for the dressing later.

Bring a large saucepan of water to a rolling boil. Carefully lower the whole eggs into the water and simmer for 6 minutes. Lift out and lower into a bowl of cold water. Carefully remove the shells, taking care not to break the eggs.

Heat the vegetable oil in a deep-fat fryer to 180°C (350°F) or in a deep heavy-based saucepan until a breadcrumb sizzles and turns brown when dropped into it. (Note: hot oil can be dangerous; do not leave unattended.) Line a tray with kitchen paper.

Spoon the flour into a shallow bowl and season well. Pour the beaten eggs into a separate, shallow bowl and the breadcrumbs into another bowl. Gently roll each peeled egg in the flour to cover all over, do the same in the beaten egg and then in the breadcrumbs, ensuring each one is completely coated.

Carefully lower 3 eggs into the hot oil and fry for about 1 minute until golden. Lift out onto the kitchen paper to drain and repeat with the other 3 eggs.

Make the dressing for the salad. Put all the ingredients into the frying pan used for the bacon and croutons, add 1 tablespoon of water and season well. Bring up to a simmer, whisking well to mix everything together.

Arrange all the salad leaves on a platter then scatter the bacon and croutons over the top. Put the eggs on a board and use a sharp knife to cut them in half lengthways. Nestle them into the salad, spoon over the warm dressing and serve.

SAUSAGE ROLLS WITH CRISPY BACON & A FRUITY DIPPING SAUCE

Using good-quality pork is key here – as a pig farmer in my younger years, I know that using cheap pork will result in too much fat and soggy pastry. The sauce is the best part of the recipe, though – I borrowed the idea from my mate, Paul Ainsworth of the Michelin-starred Number 6 restaurant in Padstow. Soak the fruit in water and blitz for just long enough to make a really smooth sauce.

SERVES 6

600g pork sausagemeat
2 egg yolks, beaten

For the sauce
300g sultanas
1 shallot, peeled and sliced
285-g bottle HP sauce

For the puff pastry
250g strong bread flour,
    plus extra to dust
1 teaspoon sea salt
125g butter, cubed,
    plus 250g butter in
    one piece

To serve
150g streaky bacon

Start by soaking the sultanas for the sauce. Place them in a heatproof bowl, pour over boiling water until they're just covered, and leave to soak.

Make the pastry. Put the flour and salt in a large bowl, add the 125g cubed butter and rub into the flour, using your fingertips, until the mixture resembles breadcrumbs. Gradually stir in 175ml cold water until you have a soft dough (you may not need all the water). Pat the dough into a 2-cm thick rectangular block, wrap it in clingfilm and chill for 30 minutes.

Roll out the dough on a lightly floured work surface until it measures around 30 x 20cm, with the longest edge lying horizontally. Put the remaining butter between two pieces of greaseproof paper and roll or bash it into a rectangle measuring 10 x 8cm. Put this in the centre of the pastry and fold one side over the butter to half-cover it, then fold the other over to cover the other half so that the two edges of pastry meet. Pinch together the top and bottom edges of the pastry to seal the butter inside. Fold the pastry in half lengthways, then turn it 90 degrees to the right (a quarter-turn). Roll out the pastry again to around 30 x 20cm. Fold the pastry as before, bringing the right side in by a third and the left edge over the top. Press the open edges together lightly and give the pastry a quarter-turn. Repeat the rolling and folding process once more, then wrap in clingfilm and chill for 1 hour.

Preheat the oven to 200°C (180°C fan)/400°F/gas 6. Cut the pastry in half and roll out each piece on a lightly floured clean work surface so that each measures 30 x 15cm rectangle. Divide the sausagemeat into two and roughly shape each into a thick sausage the length of the pastry. Place each along the centre of the lengths of pastry, then fold the pastry over the sausage, press down the edges to seal and brush with egg yolk. Transfer each roll onto a baking tray and bake for 20–25 minutes.

To make the sauce, put the sultanas plus any soaking liquor and the shallot into a pan and warm gently. Tip the mixture into a food processor, add the HP sauce and blitz until smooth. Spoon into a bowl.

Dry-fry the bacon in a large frying pan until crispy, drain on a plate lined with kitchen paper, then cut into pieces.

Slice the sausage rolls into portions, sprinkle with the crispy bacon pieces and serve with the dipping sauce.

TEMPURA MONKFISH & VEGETABLES WITH MINTED PEAS

On my travels thoughout Britain, this was the one type of fish that I saw most in fishmongers. It's often called anglerfish due to its funny-looking head, and the cheeks and tail are the bits of the fish you eat. Nowadays it's quite expensive but it was once used as a substitute for scampi when the price of langoustines was high. This is a great way to cook monkfish and the crushed minted peas are all you need with it.

SERVES 2

1–2 litres vegetable oil,
   for deep-frying
2 small carrots, halved
   lengthways
25g sugar snap peas
25g mange tout
25g marsh samphire
1 raw globe artichoke heart,
   sliced (see my tip below)
2 small courgettes, sliced
300g monkfish, cut into
   2-cm slices

For the batter
250g self-raising flour
250ml sparkling water
1 teaspoon sea salt,
   plus extra to season

For the peas
25g butter
200g frozen peas, defrosted
small bunch of mint, leaves
   picked and finely chopped

Heat the vegetable oil in a deep-fat fryer to 180°C (350°F) or in a deep heavy-based saucepan until a breadcrumb sizzles and turns brown when dropped into it. (Note: hot oil can be dangerous; do not leave unattended.) Line a large tray with kitchen paper.

Prepare the peas. Melt the butter in a medium pan over a low to medium heat and add the peas and mint. Cover and warm through for a few minutes, then use a potato masher or fork to crush the mixture slightly. Cover and keep warm.

Put all the ingredients for the batter into a large bowl and mix together until smooth. Add all the vegetables and fish then toss everything together gently to coat completely.

Use a slotted spoon to lift 8–10 pieces out of the batter and carefully lower them into the hot oil, separating them out. Fry for 1–2 minutes until golden and crisp, then drain on the kitchen paper and season with salt. Continue to cook the fish and vegetables in batches until all the pieces are cooked.

Pile the tempura monkfish and vegetables onto a plate and serve the minted peas alongside.

JAMES'S TIP

To prepare the heart from a globe artichoke, first cut the top off the artichoke, about halfway through the middle, and trim the stalk at the base. Pull off all the leaves and use a spoon to scrape out the choke. Discard the leaves and the hairy choke. Use a vegetable peeler to strip away the tough outer peel of the artichoke heart then slice. If you're not using it immediately, fill a small bowl with cold water and add a couple of slices of lemon and the artichoke heart to stop it from going brown.

ARBROATH SMOKIE SCOTCH EGGS WITH A CURRY MAYONNAISE

Arbroath Smokies – haddock cured in salt then hot-smoked in a whisky barrel – can be eaten hot or cold and are best at the markets dotted around Scotland where Mr Spink and others make them. I grabbed some at Kirkcaldy market when I made this dish on my trip but you can buy them online. Combining them with potato and wrapping them carefully around a soft-boiled egg makes an amazing-tasting dish.

SERVES 6

6 eggs, at room temperature
75g panko breadcrumbs
75g plain flour
2 eggs, beaten
8 Arbroath Smokies, skinned
    and separated into large flakes
1kg cooled mashed potato
2 litres vegetable oil, for
    deep-frying

For the curry mayonnaise
3 egg yolks
1 tablespoon Dijon mustard
1 tablespoon white wine vinegar
200ml vegetable oil
1 tablespoon mild curry powder
sea salt and freshly ground
    black pepper

Bring a large pan of water to the boil and simmer the eggs for 6 minutes. Lift out and place into a bowl of iced water. Leave for 10 minutes to cool quickly. Carefully crack the eggs and peel them.

For the curry mayonnaise, whisk the egg yolks, mustard and vinegar in a medium bowl until smooth. Slowly pour in the vegetable oil, starting with a little drizzle and whisking well. This is easiest to do with an electric hand whisk. Continue to drizzle in the remaining oil, whisking all the time, until the mixture has thickened. In a small bowl, stir 1 tablespoon of water into the curry powder and mix to make a paste. Add this to the mayonnaise, season with salt and pepper and whisk in until smooth. Cover and chill.

To assemble the Scotch eggs, put the breadcrumbs into one bowl, the flour into another, seasoning it well, and the beaten eggs into another. Stir the fish and cooled mash together in a large bowl, season and mix until smooth. Divide into 6 even-sized portions. Take one portion and flatten it into a rough disc, large enough to cover a boiled egg. Lightly flour your hands, then lay the disc in the palm of one hand, place an egg in the middle then carefully wrap it, gently pressing around it so it's sealed well. Do the same with the remaining eggs until they're all covered. Take each one and roll it in the flour, then the egg, then back into the flour and egg again. Finally roll in the breadcrumbs and gently re-shape into a sphere if necessary.

Heat the vegetable oil in a deep-fat fryer to 160°C (325°F) or in a deep heavy-based saucepan until a breadcrumb sizzles and turns brown when dropped into it. (Note: hot oil can be dangerous; do not leave unattended.) Line a large plate with kitchen paper. Use a slotted spoon to carefully lower the Scotch eggs into the hot oil and fry for 3–4 minutes until golden and crispy. Lift out and drain on the kitchen paper and season with a pinch of salt. (Cook the eggs in batches if you have a small fryer or pan.)

Serve them with a big dollop of the mayonnaise on the side.

ISLE OF WIGHT PRAWNS WITH TOMATOES, MANGALITZA CHORIZO & PANCETTA

The Hut is a hidden gem on the Isle of Wight surrounded by colourful beach huts in the sheltered Colwell Bay, Freshwater, a stone's throw from Yarmouth. It is a great place to chill out and watch the yachts moor up and the sun go down over a beer (you might need to book in advance). They cook delicious local food simply and this is my twist on one of their dishes. I used local tomatoes and garlic that thrive in the island's amazing weather (even on the 3-mile crossing over, the temperature increased by 7 degrees!) and added Mangalitza pork from just over the water in the New Forest.

SERVES 2

50ml olive oil, plus extra to drizzle
2 garlic cloves, chopped, plus
   1 extra clove, halved
½ shallot, diced
4 tomatoes, quartered
10 cherry tomatoes
3 thin slices of pancetta, chopped
6 slices of Mangalitza chorizo
   picante, chopped
½ small bunch of basil, torn
sea salt and freshly ground
   black pepper
1 red chilli, chopped
6 large prawns
2 slices of sourdough

Light your BBQ. When the coals are silvery in colour, it's ready to start cooking.

Heat a large frying pan over a medium heat for a minute or so, then add the oil, the chopped garlic, shallot and tomatoes. Stir everything together and cook for 2–3 minutes until the tomatoes have started to soften and cook down. Add the pancetta, chorizo and basil and continue to cook for another 2 minutes. Season, then add the chilli and stir it through.

Peel the shells off the prawns, leaving the heads on, drizzle over the oil and season and drizzle the bread with oil.

Pop the prawns onto the BBQ, along with the bread, and cook until they are charred. Turn over and continue to cook again until charred on the other side.

To serve, rub the charred bread with the cut clove of garlic and put a slice on each plate. Pile the tomato and chorizo mixture onto the bread and top with the prawns. (Pictured overleaf.)

CRAB CAKES WITH HOMEMADE MAYONNAISE

Brown crabs are extremely commercially important and the crab fishery in British waters is one of the largest in the world, although the bulk of crabs are still exported to Spain and France. Brown crabs are found all over the British Isles where the rocks and weeds provide cover and, of course, the cold water. I've never eaten crab as good as the ones I tasted in Cromer and in the Orkney Islands on this trip. These cakes showcase the delicious flavour of fresh crab.

SERVES 4

400g white crab meat
400g cooked potato, pushed through a ricer
6 spring onions, sliced
small bunch of chives, chopped
juice of ½ lemon
1 egg yolk
sea salt and freshly ground black pepper
25g plain flour, for dusting
olive oil, for frying

For the mayonnaise
3 egg yolks
1 tablespoon Dijon mustard
1 tablespoon white wine vinegar
200ml vegetable oil
sea salt and freshly ground black pepper

To serve
small bunch of watercress
1 lemon, cut into 4 wedges

Start by making the mayonnaise. Whisk the egg yolks, mustard and vinegar together in a medium bowl until smooth. Slowly pour the vegetable oil into the bowl, starting with a little drizzle and whisking well. This is easiest to do with an electric hand whisk. Continue to drizzle in the remaining oil, whisking all the time, until the mixture has thickened. Season to taste.

Put the crab into a large bowl with the potatoes, spring onions, chives, lemon juice and egg yolk. Season and mix everything together well. Divide the mixture into 8 portions. Dust your hands with flour and form each into a round fish-cake shape roughly measuring 8–10cm in diameter and 2cm thick.

Heat a large, non-stick frying pan over a medium heat until hot. Drizzle with a little oil and pop the fish cakes in. Cook for 2–3 minutes on each side until golden and heated through. You may need to do this in batches, depending on how big your pan is.

To serve, pop 2 crab cakes onto each plate, garnish each with watercress and a lemon wedge and serve with a dollop or a little pot of mayonnaise.

SALMON MOUSSE WITH CUCUMBER & DILL PICKLE & MELBA TOAST

The key to this mousse is the quality of the smoked salmon. It's also important not to over-whizz the mixture as it can heat up and cause it to cook and split at the same time. Melba toast was one of many dishes named after Dame Nellie Melba, a famous Australian opera singer who clearly had lots of fans. One was a certain Auguste Escoffier, one of the greatest chefs ever, who named the toast after her.

SERVES 6

650g tail-end piece smoked
   salmon, skinned
100g full-fat cream cheese
100ml double cream
juice of 1 lemon
freshly ground black pepper
4 slices of white bread
small bunch of watercress

For the pickle
50ml white wine vinegar
25g caster sugar
1 teaspoon sea salt
1 cucumber, peeled, halved,
   seeds removed and diced
small bunch of dill, leaves picked

Start by making the pickle. Pour the vinegar into a pan and stir in the sugar and salt. Heat gently to warm through and to dissolve the sugar. Add the diced cucumber and take the pan off the heat. Stir in the dill and set aside to cool and infuse.

To make the mousse, cut six 1-cm slices of smoked salmon off the opposite end to the tail, carving it away from the skin. Slice each piece in half to make 12 x 5-mm slices (2 slices per serving).

Slice the remaining salmon off the tail, roughly chop it, then put into the bowl of a food processor. Add the cream cheese, cream, lemon juice and black pepper (there's no need to add any salt here as the salmon is salty enough) and whizz for 20–30 seconds.

To make the Melba toast, preheat the grill to hot. Put the bread onto a baking tray and toast until golden. Turn over and toast the other side. Chop off the crusts using a bread knife then slice through the bread horizontally. Carefully rub the untoasted side on the board to remove any excess crumbs, then cut each piece into two triangles. Put the triangles back onto the tray, untoasted side up, and toast until golden. Keep an eye on them.

Put two slices of salmon on each plate, add a spoonful of mousse and a spoonful of pickle, and serve with slices of Melba toast and a few sprigs of watercress on the side.

BEETROOT-CURED SALMON WITH FENNEL, APPLE & RADISH SALAD

Curing a side of salmon in this way makes a great treat and dinner party dish. The beetroot not only makes it taste special but the colour will look stunning for an occasion. It looks impressive but it's easy to do and uses only a few ingredients – you can even use pre-cooked packet beetroot. The most important thing is to wrap the salmon well in clingfilm and leave it for 24 hours only, then wash and dry it and you'll have cured salmon that will keep for 3 to 4 days.

SERVES 8–10

For the salmon
400g pre-cooked (not pickled
    in vinegar) beetroot
400g table salt
200g caster sugar
1 side salmon, pin-boned
    and belly removed

For the salad
1 fennel bulb, thinly sliced
1 eating apple, thinly sliced
20 radishes, thinly sliced
small bunch of dill, chopped
5 baby pak choi, leaves separated

For the dressing
100ml olive oil
juice of 2 lemons
sea salt and freshly ground
    black pepper

Put the beetroot, salt and sugar into a large food processor and blitz until smooth.

Line a large tray with several layers of clingfilm – the tray needs to be big enough to fit the salmon on and the clingfilm layers large enough to wrap around the coated salmon.

Pour half of the beetroot mixture into the tray and spread it out, leaving a border. Position the salmon on top then cover with the remaining beetroot mixture. Wrap tightly in the clingfilm, so the beetroot cure is covering all of the salmon, and transfer to the fridge to chill for 24 hours.

Remove the clingfilm and scrape off the beetroot cure. Rinse the salmon under cold running water to wash away any remaining beetroot cure, then pat dry with a clean tea towel. Transfer to a chopping board.

Make the salad by combining all the ingredients in a large bowl. Whisk the ingredients for the dressing in a separate bowl and season well, then pour over the salad and toss together.

Use a sharp fish knife to carve thin slices of the salmon, starting from the tail end, and arrange a few slices on each plate with a spoonful of the salad to accompany it. (Pictured overleaf.)

BBQ HERRING WITH SALSA

Herring are rarely seen in supermarkets other than when turned into kippers, but they are fantastic when fresh, either barbecued or simply grilled. There are a few fresh fish shops dotted along Folkestone harbour selling herring straight from the boats to the public and to restaurants, so I wanted to cook these on the beach outside Mark Sargeant's restaurant, Rocksalt.

SERVES 4

4 whole herring,
    scaled and gutted
2 tablespoons olive oil,
    plus extra to drizzle
zest of 1 lime

For the salsa
3 medium tomatoes,
    cut into chunks
1 shallot, finely diced
1 garlic clove, chopped
50ml cider vinegar
50ml olive oil
sea salt and freshly ground
    black pepper
small bunch of flat-leaf
    parsley, chopped
2 tablespoons capers
¼ baguette, torn into chunks

Light your BBQ. When the coals are silvery in colour, it will be ready to cook on.

Meanwhile make the salsa. Put the tomatoes into a bowl and add the shallot, garlic, cider vinegar and olive oil. Season well and stir everything together. Add the chopped parsley, capers and bread and stir to combine.

To prepare the herring, place them on a chopping board and cut off and discard the heads. Working on one of them, open the fish out slightly, skin side up, and press down on the backbone using the heel of your hand to flatten. Turn the fish over and gently ease the backbone out, along with the other finer bones. Cut out the end of the backbone at the tail. Do the same to the other three fish.

Drizzle the oil over the skin of all the herrings, then pop them onto the BBQ, skin-side down, and cook for 2 minutes. Flip over and cook for a further minute.

To serve, spoon the salsa onto a large plate, put the fish alongside, then finish with another drizzle of oil and sprinkle over the lime zest.

BAKED SARDINE TART WITH INDIAN CHUTNEY

I love sardines and when they're fresh it's so easy to remove the bones to make them easier for you to eat. Just pushing down on the back will free up the rib-cage bones underneath and you'll be able to just lift and pull them out (see my tip below). The combination of spices I used for this dish was inspired by a trip to Bristol, one of many British cities with an up-and-coming modern food scene.

SERVES 6

a little plain flour, for dusting
500g puff pastry
2 egg yolks, beaten
12 sardines, scaled, cleaned and butterflied (see my tip below)
10 slices of streaky bacon
olive oil, for drizzling
sea salt and freshly ground black pepper

For the chutney
2 Bramley apples, cored and diced
2 pears, diced
15g butter
5-cm piece fresh root ginger, grated
1 shallot, diced
2 garlic cloves, grated
1 teaspoon dried curry leaves
1 teaspoon garam masala
seeds from 4 cardamom pods
1 teaspoon ground cumin
1 teaspoon mild chilli powder
2 star anise

Preheat the oven to 200°C (180°C fan)/400°F/gas 6.

Start by making the chutney. Put the apples and pears into a large saucepan, add the butter and 100ml water and place over a medium heat on the hob. Bring to the boil, then stir in the ginger, shallot, garlic and curry leaves.

Put the dry spices into a small bowl, add 1 tablespoon of water and mix to a paste. Add this to the pan, together with the star anise, and stir in. Reduce the heat to a simmer and cook for 10 minutes, stirring occasionally.

To make the tart, lightly dust a clean work surface with a little flour. Roll out the pastry to make a rectangle measuring 30 x 20cm and around 2mm thick. Prick the pastry all over with a fork and lift onto a flat baking sheet.

Use a pastry brush to brush the beaten egg all over the pastry then arrange the sardines over the top, followed by the bacon. Drizzle over the olive oil, season and bake for 20–25 minutes until the pastry has puffed up and is golden and crisp.

Spoon the chutney into a bowl (remove the star anise). Slide the tart onto a board, slice into pieces and serve.

JAMES'S TIP

To prepare the sardines, put them on a board and use a scaler to remove the scales. Next, use a sharp fish knife to cut the heads off each one (or you can leave them on, as I did) then slice the knife along the belly to open them up. Pull out and discard the guts, clean any blood with tissue and rinse briefly with cold water.

Open out each sardine, flesh-side down, and use the heel of your hand to press down along the centre until each fish is flat. Turn over and gently pull out the backbone starting from the top and slicing it off at the tail.

FISH

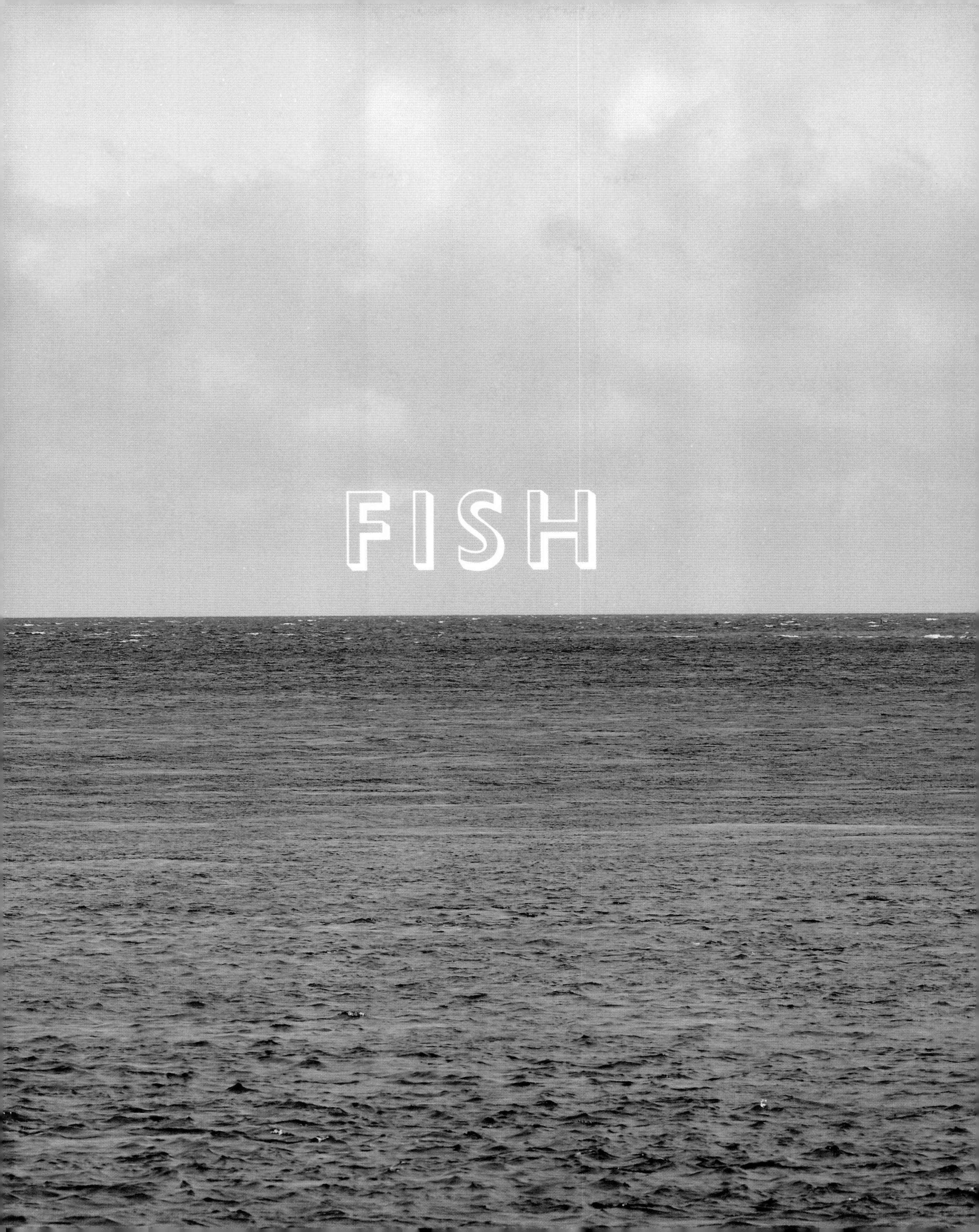

MACKEREL & CAULIFLOWER WITH MANGO DRESSING

This is such a simple dish but it relies on using top-quality and extremely fresh mackerel. Oily fish needs to be really fresh as the oils start to break down the flesh the older it is. The fruity dressing goes brilliantly here and young nasturtium leaves, if you have them, add a great peppery kick.

SERVES 4

4 whole mackerel, gutted
    and heads removed
25m olive oil
juice of 1½ lemons,
    plus 2 lemons, halved
sea salt and freshly ground
    black pepper
2 mangoes
1 tablespoon cider vinegar
125g butter
½ cauliflower, cut into florets
1 teaspoon mild curry powder

To serve
a few herb leaves and flowers
    (such as bergamot, thyme,
    nasturtium and fennel)
a few watercress leaves

Preheat the oven to 220°C (200°C fan)/425°F/gas 7.

Place the mackerel on a baking tray and score four crosses along the fillet from the top to the tail on one side. Drizzle the oil over the top, then pour over the juice of 1 lemon. Place the lemon halves on the tray and season the mackerel. Roast for 8–10 minutes until the flesh is opaque and the fillets are coming away from the central bone.

Slice down each side of the stone of each of the mangoes to remove the cheeks. Scoop the flesh into a liquidiser or food processor and add the cider vinegar. Blitz until very smooth.

Heat a large frying pan until hot. Add the butter and once it's melted and foaming, cook the cauliflower florets over a high heat for 3–4 minutes until golden and charred slightly on one side.

Take the pan off the heat, stir in the curry powder, pour over the remaining lemon juice and season and toss everything together. Lift the cauliflower onto kitchen paper to drain slightly.

Squeeze a roasted lemon half over each mackerel then lay the fish on warmed plates. Spoon the mango sauce in a line down the side. Arrange the cauliflower on top of the sauce and decorate with the edible herb leaves and flowers and watercress. Serve straightaway.

TIKKA MACKEREL BUNS WITH FENNEL & APPLE SALAD

Mackerel is one fish that we should eat a whole lot more of – it's so abundant and when eaten fresh it's one of the best-tasting. As an oily fish, it can take these strong tikka flavours and it went down well with the crowd watching on the bandstand when we were filming in Whitby (famous for its fish and chips, Captain Cook's HMS *Endeavour* and for kippers, which you can buy online from Fortune's Smokehouse).

SERVES 6

2 teaspoons ground coriander
2 teaspoons ground cumin
2 teaspoons garlic powder
1 teaspoon smoked paprika
1 tablespoon garam masala
1 teaspoon ground ginger
1 teaspoon dried mint
1 teaspoon chilli powder
250ml full-fat Greek yogurt
sea salt and freshly ground
    black pepper
small bunch of mint, leaves
    picked and chopped
small bunch of coriander,
    chopped
6 fresh curry leaves
6 mackerel fillets, pin-boned
6 brioche buns, halved
1 bag of salad leaves

For the salad
2 pickled onions, sliced
½ fennel, thinly sliced
½ green apple, julienned
juice of 1 lime
olive oil

Light your BBQ. When the coals are silvery in colour, it will be ready to cook on.

Put the ground coriander, cumin, garlic powder, smoked paprika, garam masala, ginger, mint, chilli powder and Greek yogurt in a large bowl. Mix everything together then season and add half the fresh mint, all the coriander and the curry leaves and stir to combine.

Spread a third of the mixture on a large sheet of foil. Lay the mackerel fillets on top and spread the remainder of the mixture over the top. Place another piece of foil over and seal the edges to make a parcel, then lift onto the BBQ to cook for 10 minutes.

Meanwhile, mix the pickled onions, fennel, apple and remaining mint in a bowl and pour over the lime juice to make the salad. Add a splash of olive oil, season, and mix together.

To serve, fill the buns with the salad leaves, top with a mackerel fillet and spoon over the fennel and apple salad.

BLOW-TORCHED MACKEREL WITH FENNEL & GRAPEFRUIT SALAD

I had my work cut out with this one, trying to fillet the fish and cook it on the back of a fishing boat while bobbing up and down in the sea off Northern Ireland! It was worth it, though, because the coastline around here is ruggedly beautiful with places like the Giant's Causeway and stunning villages untouched by time. I told the crew that when we were in the right place, they would see how easy mackerel are to fish for – we caught 9 in less than 4 minutes.

SERVES 2

1 tablespoon caster sugar
1 teaspoon pink peppercorns, lightly crushed
3-cm piece fresh ginger, peeled and grated
a few dill sprigs, chopped
sea salt
50ml white wine vinegar
1 pink grapefruit
½ medium fennel bulb, thinly sliced
freshly ground black pepper
1 tablespoon olive oil
4 mackerel fillets, skin on

For the dressing
100ml full-fat crème fraîche
1-cm piece fresh ginger, peeled and grated
sea salt and freshly ground black pepper

Put the sugar, peppercorns, ginger, dill and 1 teaspoon of salt into a medium bowl then stir in the vinegar.

On a board, slice the top and bottom off the grapefruit then carefully cut away the skin and pith from the fruit. Cut between each segment and add the flesh to the bowl, reserving all the juices and pouring these into the bowl, too. Add the fennel and any fronds to the bowl. Season with a little black pepper and toss everything together.

Rub the oil over the mackerel and season well. Pop the fillets, skin-side up, onto a baking sheet. Using a blow torch, scorch the skin of the mackerel until charred and the fish is cooked through. Alternatively, preheat the grill to its highest setting and cook the fish for 3–4 minutes.

Mix the crème fraîche and ginger together in a bowl with a little seasoning to make the dressing.

To serve, spoon some dressing onto each plate, lay 2 mackerel fillets on top and half of the salad alongside each.

BBQ JOHN DORY WITH KOHLRABI & FENNEL SALAD

Jonny, my mate at Flying Fish Seafoods in Cornwall, has some of the best fish available and to prove it I got the crew to go there and film all the amazing fish for sale. Sadly, the public can't buy from him but it is like a fish showroom of what's in the seas around Britain. He is passionate about his produce and those who buy from him are a 'who's who' of the country's best chefs and restaurants. One of the chefs' favourite fish has to be John Dory, as it's meaty and tastes amazing, but be careful not to overcook it.

SERVES 2

1 whole John Dory (around 1kg),
   gutted and cleaned
sea salt and freshly ground
   black pepper
100g potted shrimps
small bunch of dill,
   roughly chopped
small bunch of chives,
   roughly chopped
1 tablespoon rapeseed oil

For the salad
1 kohlrabi, thinly sliced
½ fennel bulb, thinly sliced
   (fronds reserved)
½ red onion, peeled and
   thinly sliced
6 cherry tomatoes, quartered
1 green tomato, cut into
   eight wedges
¼ cucumber, thinly sliced
   into rounds

For the dressing
1 tablespoon grainy mustard
50ml rapeseed oil
25ml white wine vinegar

Light your BBQ. When the coals are silvery in colour, it will be ready to cook on.

To prepare the fish, use scissors to snip off the fins and tail if the fishmonger hasn't already done so. Season inside the cavity then fill the fish with a quarter of the shrimps, half the chopped dill and chives and half of the fennel fronds (from the salad). Season the whole fish, drizzle with oil and rub it all over the skin, then pop onto the BBQ to cook for 6–8 minutes on each side.

For the dressing, put the mustard, oil and vinegar into a bowl. Season and whisk together to combine.

Spoon the remaining potted shrimps into a small pan and heat gently to melt the butter.

Mix the kohlrabi, fennel, red onion, both types of tomato, the cucumber and the remaining dill, chives and fennel fronds into a large bowl. Drizzle over the dressing and toss everything together.

To serve, pile the salad on the side of a large platter and pop the fish alongside. Spoon the hot potted shrimp and any buttery juices over the fish and serve. (Pictured overleaf.)

PAN-FRIED COD WITH A WARM TARTARE SAUCE

Large line-caught cod are one of the true delicacies of the cold waters around Britain; the smaller trawler-caught fish are mainly from the waters further north and are used for the fish and chip industry. A nice chunk of cod simply cooked is a delight with a warm tartare sauce. This is simple to make, but take care not to boil the sauce as the eggs in the mayonnaise will start to curdle.

SERVES 2

40g butter
sea salt and freshly ground
    black pepper
2 x 150-g skinless cod fillets
200g cooked Maris Piper
    potatoes, diced
50g fresh podded or frozen peas
bunch of asparagus
100g samphire

For the tartare sauce
50ml hot fish stock
100ml double cream
1 tablespoon fresh mayonnaise
1 little gem lettuce, shredded
4 baby gherkins, diced
1 teaspoon nonpareille capers
a few dill fronds, chopped
50g white Cromer crab meat
juice of ½ lemon

Heat a non-stick frying pan over a medium heat until hot then add 15g of the butter. Season the cod and as soon as the butter has melted, add the fillets to the pan and cook for 2–3 minutes on one side. Carefully turn them over and cook for a further 2–3 minutes, until the fish is opaque all the way through. Lift onto a warm plate, then cover and rest. Set the pan aside to use for the sauce.

Pop the remaining butter into a separate medium saucepan and place over a medium heat. As soon as the butter has melted, stir in the potatoes and peas. Cut the asparagus spears in half and dice the bottom half of the stems. Add these to the pan together with the samphire. Season well and cook, stirring everything together, for 2–3 minutes.

To make the tartare sauce, pour the stock and cream into the frying pan the fish was cooked in. Bring to the boil, then reduce the heat to a gentle simmer. Add the mayonnaise, lettuce, gherkins, capers, dill and crab meat. Season well then stir in the lemon juice, mixing everything together.

To serve, divide the potato, pea and asparagus mixture between two warmed bowls, top each with a portion of cod and spoon the warm tartare sauce over the top.

PAN-FRIED PLAICE WITH LANGOUSTINES

If there was one thing I would choose for food heaven it would be this fish and fresh langoustines. For years in this country we've mainly enjoyed langoustines breaded and deep fried as scampi. The best scampi, by the way, is at The Stapylton Arms in Wass, Yorkshire – you need to visit and try them. Rob works behind the hobs and Gill works the front of house in this classic pub which also offers good beer and great steak.

SERVES 4

24 langoustines, cooked and shelled (shells reserved)
2 shallots, sliced
½ head of celery, chopped
½ leek, chopped
12 black peppercorns
50ml double cream
sea salt and freshly ground black pepper
4 x 150-g plaice fillets
25ml olive oil
50g butter
juice of 1 lemon
50ml champagne
small bunch of flat-leaf parsley, chopped

To make a stock, put the langoustine shells into a large pan, bash them with a rolling pin to break them up a little bit, then pour in 1 litre of cold water.

Cover the pan and bring to the boil, then add the shallots, celery, leek and peppercorns and simmer for 10 minutes.

Strain the stock through a fine sieve into a clean, hot pan, bring to the boil and simmer until it's reduced by half. Pour in the cream and simmer until the sauce has reduced by half again.

Heat a large, non-stick frying pan over a medium heat until hot. Season the plaice fillets on the underside.

Drizzle the oil into the pan and add half of the butter. When the butter is foaming, add the fish and cook on one side for 1 minute. Add half of the remaining butter, then turn the fish over and cook for a further 30 seconds. Lift onto a plate lined with kitchen paper to drain and cover to keep warm.

Using the same pan, gently heat the langoustines and lemon juice to warm through.

Finish the sauce by keeping the pan over a low to medium heat and stirring in the remaining butter. Pour in the champagne and stir in the parsley, reserving a little for garnish. Season to taste.

To serve, spoon the sauce onto each warmed plate, pop the plaice on top, spoon the langoustines over and sprinkle with a little parsley.

PLAICE WITH CRAB FRITTERS

This recipe uses the same mixture as a choux pastry for desserts like éclairs but when mixed with crab and deep fried it makes a great snack or garnish to a main course. These fritters go brilliantly with fresh fish roasted on the bone to keep all the flavour and moisture in. Billingsgate Fish Market in London used to sell 30 million plaice a year at the height of the fish's popularity but it is often overlooked these days. It is available all year round, but I find it is best from summer to mid-winter. It's an amazing-tasting fish if cooked simply, as here.

SERVES 4

1 large plaice (fins, skirt
   and tail removed)
vegetable oil, for greasing
15g butter

For the crab fritters
85g butter, diced
115g strong plain bread flour
400g brown crab meat
3 medium eggs
a pinch of sea salt
1–2 litres vegetable oil,
   for deep-frying

For the sauce
100ml dry white wine
200g white crab meat
100ml double cream
sea salt and freshly ground
   black pepper
75g butter
juice of ½ lemon

For the samphire
10g butter
200g samphire

Preheat the oven to 200°C (180°C fan)/400°F/gas 6.

Put the plaice on a chopping board, with the head facing away from you. Carefully cut down one side of the central bone and work the knife against the fish bones to release the fillet, but don't cut all the way through – it should still be attached. Do the same on the other side. Open out the fillets so they lie flat on either side of the fish. Lift onto an oiled roasting tray, dot with the butter and roast for 15–20 minutes, until the fish is opaque and the central bone lifts away from the flesh. If there is any pink flesh around the bone, continue to cook, checking every 2–3 minutes.

To make the crab fritters, pour 200ml water into a medium saucepan and add the butter. Place over a medium heat and as soon as the butter has melted, bring to a rolling boil. Add the flour and beat well for about 1 minute over the heat until smooth. Take the pan off the heat and cool slightly, then stir in the crab. Beat in the eggs, one by one, until the dough is smooth and glossy, then stir in the salt.

For the sauce, put the wine, crab meat and cream into a pan, stir together and season. Place over a medium heat and bring to the boil. Add the butter and lemon juice and as soon as the butter has melted, take off the heat and blitz with a stick blender. Cover and keep warm.

Heat the vegetable oil in a deep-fat fryer to 200°C (400°F) or in a deep, heavy-based saucepan until a breadcrumb sizzles and turns brown when dropped into it. (Note: hot oil can be dangerous; do not leave unattended.) Line a tray with kitchen paper. Lower heaped tablespoons of fritter mixture into the hot oil, frying in batches of 3–4 for approximately 2 minutes, until golden and crispy. Lift onto the lined tray and season with salt.

Finally, cook the samphire. Heat the butter and 25ml water in a medium pan until the butter has melted. Add the samphire, season well and cook for 1 minute.

Lift the fish onto a platter, top with the crab fritters then scatter over the samphire. Drizzle with the sauce and serve.

SEAWEED-DEEP-FRIED PLAICE WITH BROWN CRAB MAYONNAISE & LEMON

This was the last dish I cooked on the road trip and it was probably the one I was looking forward to the most. The crew didn't make it easy for me, perched on a rock face overlooking Padstow and Rock, but it seemed the right place to cook it, mainly because I had access to incredible fish and the dried dulse seaweed that works as a seasoning in this batter. Using the brown crab meat in the mayo is something I do back in the restaurant; it's easier to make there, too, but with the help of my mate and great cook Paul Ainsworth (see page 28), this was one of my and the filmcrew's favourites.

SERVES 3

6 plaice fillets
1–2 litres vegetable oil,
    for deep-frying
1 lemon, cut into 6 wedges

For the batter
250g plain flour
1 tablespoon bicarbonate
    of soda
½ teaspoon sea salt
1 tablespoon dulse
    seaweed powder
250ml sparkling water

For the mayonnaise
3 egg yolks
1 tablespoon Dijon mustard
200ml vegetable oil
100g brown crab meat
juice of ½ lemon
sea salt and freshly ground
    black pepper

Start by making the mayonnaise. Whisk the egg yolks and Dijon mustard together in a large bowl until smooth. Slowly pour the vegetable oil into the bowl, starting with a little drizzle and whisking well. This is easiest to do with an electric hand whisk. Continue to drizzle in the remaining oil, whisking all the time, until the mixture has thickened. Stir in the brown crab meat and lemon juice and season to taste.

Heat the vegetable oil in a deep-fat fryer to 180°C (350°F) or in a deep, heavy-based saucepan until a breadcrumb sizzles and turns brown when dropped into it. (Note: hot oil can be dangerous; do not leave unattended.) Line a plate or tray with kitchen paper.

Sift the flour, bicarbonate of soda and salt into a large bowl. Stir in the seaweed then slowly pour in the sparkling water, whisking well until you have a smooth batter.

Lower 3 of the fish fillets into the batter and toss to coat, making sure they're completely covered, then use tongs to lift them out and carefully lower them into the hot oil. Cook for 2 minutes, until golden and crispy, then lift onto the kitchen paper and season with salt. Batter and fry the remaining fish.

Spoon the mayonnaise into a bowl and serve 2 fish fillets and 2 lemon wedges per person. (Pictured overleaf.)

GURNARD & RED MULLET WITH ORANGE-CHARRED CHICORY & CAULIFLOWER PURÉE

I first came across red mullet in French markets and on the menus when I was training over there. It's a fish that's mainly caught around the east, west and south coasts, like the gurnard – both have an amazing flavour and can take quite strong garnishes like this chicory. If you want to push the boat out, cooked red mullet liver tastes great spread over toast. The gurnard is an Atlantic and Mediterranean ocean fish; it's a prehistoric-looking thing with big, red winged gills and is good value.

SERVES 2

2 green chicory bulbs
1 red chicory bulb
1 tablespoon olive oil,
    plus extra for drizzling
1 tablespoon caster sugar
zest of 1 orange, juice of 2
25g sultanas
a few thyme sprigs
200ml chicken stock
sea salt and freshly ground
    black pepper
50g butter
1 small cauliflower, 6 leaves
    separated and florets chopped
500ml milk
2 x 100-g gurnard fillets
2 x 100-g red mullet fillets

Cut each chicory bulb in half lengthways. Heat a large, non-stick frying pan over a medium heat until hot. Drizzle the cut sides of the chicory with oil and pop them in, cut-side down. Cook until charred. Sprinkle over the caster sugar and cook until the sugar caramelises.

Add the orange zest, orange juice, sultanas and thyme and pour over the stock. Season well and simmer over a medium heat until the sauce has reduced by half. Finish with a third of the butter, shaking the pan slightly once it's melted.

Put the cauliflower florets into a medium saucepan with the milk. Cook over a gentle heat until the cauliflower is soft, then blitz in a liquidiser or use a stick blender to whizz in the pan until smooth. Season and add half the remaining butter. Pour into a clean pan over a very low heat to keep warm.

Heat 1 tablespoon of olive oil in a large frying pan and add the last of the butter. Once the butter has melted and starts to foam, place the gurnard fillets in, skin-side down, season and cook for 2 minutes. Add the mullet fillets, again skin-side down, season and cook for another minute then flip all the fillets over. Add the cauliflower leaves and cook for another minute.

To serve, spoon the cauliflower purée onto 2 plates, then 3 halves of the chicory onto each. Top with a fillet of each fish and the cauliflower leaves and drizzle over the sauce.

DOVER SOLE WITH BROWN BUTTER & WATERCRESS

Simply, simply, simply is the way you need to cook Dover sole. It is one of the best fish out there and sadly, like so much other fish we catch in this country, it gets immediately exported. Best caught off the south coast from Dover round to Hastings, it's a delicate fish that we should enjoy more often. It is delicious cooked whole and on the bone and eaten with brown butter to add a touch of bitterness to the dish. This is a real chef's favourite to eat, I promise.

SERVES 2

2 tablespoons plain flour
sea salt and freshly ground
  black pepper
1 Dover sole, filleted
3 tablespoons olive oil
200g butter
juice of 1 lemon
small bunch of flat-leaf
  parsley, chopped

To serve
small bunch of watercress

Line a sieve with muslin and rest it over a bowl. Spoon the flour into a shallow dish and season well. Dip the fish fillets into the flour and coat well, then shake briefly to dust off any excess.

Heat a large, non-stick frying pan over a medium heat until hot. Add the oil, swirl it around to heat it, then lay the sole fillets into the pan. Cook the fish for 1–2 minutes until golden (you may need to lower the heat slightly at this stage, so the pan doesn't become too hot) then flip the fillets over and cook on the other side for 1–2 minutes more. Pop onto a warmed plate.

Put the pan back over a medium heat and add the butter. Cook until the butter turns nut brown – it's ready when it smells nutty – then take the pan immediately off the heat and strain through the muslin-lined sieve. Stir the lemon juice and parsley into the butter in the bowl, then spoon over the fish and serve straightaway with the watercress alongside.

MARLOES SANDS SEAFOOD PARCEL

Just a stone's throw from St Davids, Marloes Sands was one of many places I hadn't been before I started this trip and, like the others, it didn't disappoint. The coastline here in Wales is beautiful and looks even better from a sea canoe, bobbing up and down in search of rock samphire. This stretch of beach is owned by the National Trust, though, so don't go picking any – it is always best to go foraging with a guide who can run through what you can and can't eat. It is really fascinating to see what is out there along our shores and in the countryside.

SERVES 4

100g smoked back bacon,
   cut into 1-cm strips
600g haddock, cut into 4 pieces
1 teaspoon dried dulse flakes
1 teaspoon dried kelp flakes
50g cockles in their shells,
   cleaned
4 whole medium raw prawns
1 medium courgette,
   cut into batons
12 cherry tomatoes, halved
a few sprigs of dill, leaves picked
25g butter, cubed
sea salt and freshly ground
   black pepper

To serve
crusty bread

Light your BBQ. When the coals are silvery in colour, it's ready to start cooking.

Heat a medium frying pan over a medium heat and dry-fry the bacon until crispy. Lift onto a plate and set aside.

Tear two large squares of foil, approximately 30 x 30cm, then tear the same sized pieces of baking parchment and lay on top of each square of foil.

Put two pieces of haddock into the middle of each square and sprinkle over the dulse and kelp seaweed. Add all the other ingredients, dividing them equally between the two squares, and season well. Pour 1 tablespoon of water over each then bring the foil up and around the ingredients and seal well.

Place the parcels onto the BBQ and cook for 8–10 minutes, then open each parcel to check everything's cooked – the haddock should be opaque, the cockles should have opened and the prawns should have turned pink.

Unwrap each parcel and divide each between two plates. Serve with plenty of crusty bread to dip in the delicious juices.

BLAIR CASTLE SALMON WITH SAFFRON SAUCE

Salmon fishing with Tom Kitchin was a must on this trip but, like my days of fishing on Scottish rivers in previous years, it had the same result: nothing. We had just driven back from a massive trek up the glen and spent the afternoon on the Tay in search of one of Scotland's elusive (to me, anyway) wild salmon. Still, there can be few things more uplifting than a day in the Scottish Highlands when the weather is stunning.

SERVES 4

25ml rapeseed oil
sea salt and freshly ground
    black pepper
4 x 200-g salmon fillets, skin on
1 shallot, diced
1 medium fennel bulb, sliced
1 garlic clove, diced
12 cherry tomatoes, halved
50ml dry white wine
250g mussels, cleaned and
    debearded (see my tip below)
100g langoustine tails
100g crayfish, shelled
100ml double cream
pinch of saffron
small bunch of chives, chopped
small bunch of flat-leaf
    parsley, chopped

Heat a large, flat griddle pan over a medium to high heat until hot, then drizzle with half the oil. Season the salmon fillets all over and pop on the griddle, skin-side down. Cook for 3–4 minutes then turn over and cook for a further 2 minutes. Set aside on a plate and cover to keep warm.

In a separate large, heavy-based saucepan, heat the remaining oil and add the shallot, fennel, garlic and tomatoes and sauté for 4–5 minutes, until softened but not coloured. Season well then pour in the wine. Add the mussels, langoustines and crayfish, then cover the pan and cook for 2–3 minutes until the mussels have steamed open. Discard any that remain closed.

Pour the cream into the pan, add the saffron and season again. Cover and cook for 2 minutes more, then add the chopped herbs and stir through. Ladle the sauce and shellfish into four shallow bowls and top each with a salmon fillet.

JAMES'S TIP

Fresh mussels need to be alive before you cook them. Throw away any with broken shells or any that don't close tightly when you tap them. To prepare mussels, pull off the stringy beards, scrape off any barnacles and give the shells a scrub in fresh water to clean them.

GIANT'S CAUSEWAY FISH STEW

I don't know who looked more confused, me or the thousands of tourists all around me while we were filming this dish on the stones of the Giant's Causeway. I'd never been before but it really is a sight to behold. In fact, the whole coastline of this part of Northern Ireland is worth a trip – it is rugged and beautiful in equal measure, as is the produce that can be found here. Ales, meat, dairy, fish... It is so rich and diverse with such amazing food.

SERVES 6

400g mussels, cleaned and debearded (see my tip on page 82)
25g butter
1 shallot, finely diced
25g plain flour
sea salt and freshly ground black pepper
400ml full-fat milk
100ml double cream
1 medium floury potato, cooked and diced (you need 200g)
400g salmon fillet, skinned and chopped into 2-cm cubes
200g white crab meat
100g brown crab meat
small bunch of chives, chopped

To serve
double cream
olive oil

Place a large sieve over a bowl. Pour 100ml water into a large heavy-based saucepan and set the pan over a high heat. Add the mussels, cover with a lid and cook for 3 minutes until the mussels have steamed open. Strain the mussels through the sieve, reserving the liquor, then pick the mussel meat from the shells and set aside. Discard any mussels that haven't opened.

In the same pan, melt the butter over a medium heat. As soon as the butter has melted, stir in the shallot and cook for 1–2 minutes, stirring regularly, until softened.

Stir in the flour, season, and cook for around 1 minute. Pour the reserved mussel liquor into the pan, stirring all the time, then add the milk and cream. Bring to a gentle simmer, stirring continuously, until smooth.

Add the potato and salmon, stir everything together, then cover the pan and cook for 2–3 minutes until the potatoes are hot and the salmon has cooked through.

Stir in both types of crab meat and the mussel meat and warm through for a couple of minutes. Add a couple of tablespoons of hot water if the sauce is very thick. Season to taste and scatter over most of the chives.

To serve, ladle the stew into warmed bowls, drizzle with a little extra cream and olive oil, if you fancy, and garnish with the remaining chives.

FOLKESTONE FISH

The guys at Folkstone Trawlers are first-rate fishermen who supply restaurants and their little shop by the harbour. We waited there, early doors, to get the fresh catch and, with other boats bringing in different shellfish, I jumped at the chance to get a few bits of local fish to cook with. Sadly, nowadays most people buy fresh fish from supermarkets but if you have a stall or fresh fish shop near you, do use them as they need your support and the quality is usually brilliant. Plus, asking about the fish from the people who catch them is always best.

SERVES 2

1 whole lemon sole
2 monkfish fillets (around
    200g in total)
sea salt and freshly ground
    black pepper
2 tablespoons olive oil
25g butter, plus an extra
    knob to finish
1 shallot, diced
1 garlic clove, crushed
100ml dry cider
200g mussels, cleaned and
    debearded (see my tip
    on page 82)
pinch of saffron
100ml double cream
small bunch of flat-leaf
    parsley, chopped

Heat a large non-stick pan over a medium heat until hot.

Place the sole on a board and, using a pair of scissors, cut off and discard the fins. Use a sharp fish knife to remove the head (discard it), then cut the fish into 3 darnes and set aside on the board. Cut the monkfish into 5-cm chunks. Season all of the fish.

Pour the oil into the pan and add the butter. When the butter has melted and starts to foam, pop all the fish into the pan, spaced apart, and cook for 2 minutes. Flip the pieces of fish over and cook for a further 2 minutes, then transfer to a warm plate.

Keep the pan over a low to medium heat and add the shallot and garlic. Stir together and cook for about 1 minute, then pour in the cider and bring to the boil. Add the mussels to the pan, then add the saffron and pour in the cream. Stir everything together, cover the pan with a lid and cook for 2 minutes. Check all the mussels have opened; discard any that haven't.

Remove the lid, add the fish to the pan to warm it through, then sprinkle over some chopped parsley and season well. To finish, stir in the remaining knob of butter. Divide between two bowls, spooning any buttery juices over the top.

SHELLFISH

LOBSTER WITH WHITE PORT & REDCURRANT JELLY

I cooked this on a riverboat passing the legendary three Michelin-star Waterside Inn at Bray, the place that helped put Britain on the international food scene. Opened by Michel and Albert Roux in the 1970s, the restaurant inspired local press to ask what the French were doing here. Looking at the team members who work and have worked there over the years, we can see it has fed the British food scene with more than just a restaurant – very few places can claim such a legacy. This dish is iconic. End of.

SERVES 2

100ml white port
100ml fish stock
300ml veal jus
1 cooked lobster, meat removed
    and shells reserved
65g butter
a pinch of cayenne
sea salt and freshly ground
    black pepper
5-cm piece fresh ginger, julienned
    (sliced into thin matchsticks)
2 carrots, julienned
1 leek, julienned
2 tablespoons redcurrant jelly
3-4 sprigs of chervil, to garnish

To make the sauce, pour the port, fish stock and veal jus into a medium pan. Add the lobster shells and bring to the boil. Lower the heat to a simmer and cook until the liquid reduces to a third. Discard the lobster shells. Whisk in 50g of the butter and season with the cayenne and salt and pepper. Set aside and keep warm.

Heat the remaining butter in a sauté pan. When the butter has melted, add the julienned ginger, carrot and leek and 1 tablespoon of water and sauté until just soft. Add the lobster meat and redcurrant jelly and season well. Heat gently to melt the jelly and warm the lobster through for a couple of minutes. You may need to add another tablespoon of water to help dissolve the jelly.

Spoon the vegetables and lobster onto two warmed plates and spoon over the sauce. Garnish with chervil to serve.

HOMEMADE CRUMPETS WITH BUTTERED LOBSTER, SPINACH & SAMPHIRE

What a day we had filming at the oldest fighter squadron in the world: No.1 Squadron at RAF Lossiemouth. They wanted lobster on the menu, so their wish was my command, especially when they let me loose in the simulator of a Typhoon jet. But the best was yet to come when they let me fly a stunning old taildragger down the runway, up and over the lighthouse and around at a few 100 feet over the town.

SERVES 8

175g strong white bread flour
175g plain flour
2 x 7g sachets easy bake
  dried yeast
1 teaspoon caster sugar
½ teaspoon bicarbonate soda
1 teaspoon salt
350ml full-fat milk, warmed
100ml warm water
a little butter for greasing
  and frying

For the topping
100g butter
600g cooked lobster meat
200g baby spinach
200g samphire
sea salt and freshly ground
  black pepper
nutmeg, for seasoning

You will need
8 crumpet rings (or 4 if
  cooking in 2 batches)

Tip both types of flour into a large bowl. Add the remaining crumpet ingredients, apart from the butter, and whisk together until smooth. Cover and leave to prove in a warm place for 2–3 hours.

Heat a large, flat griddle pan over a medium heat until hot. Lightly butter the inside of the crumpet rings, then brush the pan with butter and arrange the crumpet rings over it, spaced apart. Work in two batches if there isn't enough space on the griddle pan to cook all the crumpets in one go.

Pour the batter into the buttered rings and cook over a medium heat for 3 minutes. Carefully remove the rings using a palette knife and flip the crumpets over. Cook for a further 2 minutes then transfer to a plate and keep warm.

For the topping, melt the butter in the same pan and add the lobster to warm through for a couple of minutes. Add the spinach and samphire and turn over in the heat until it wilts. Season well, grate over a little nutmeg and stir in.

To serve, pop a crumpet onto each plate and spoon over some of the lobster and greens.

ORKNEY CRAB PASTA

I might get in trouble as I travel around Britain for saying this but the crab I had in Orkney was the very best I've ever tasted. Don't just take my word for it – Nick Nairn, who's from Scotland, had never tasted it before and he agreed. We also tasted the best vinegar here too, and I nearly bought an island! I loved the Orkneys – it's a very, very special place. And the ingredients around here are both pure and some of the very best.

SERVES 4–6

400g fresh tagliatelle pasta
1 tablespoon olive oil
2 shallots, chopped
3 garlic cloves, chopped
100ml dry white wine
100g brown crab meat
50ml double cream
200g white crab meat
1 red chilli, chopped
1 green chilli, chopped
zest and juice of 1 lemon
small bunch of flat-leaf
  parsley, chopped
sea salt and freshly ground
  black pepper

Bring a large pan of salted water to the boil, add the pasta and cook following the packet instructions, until al dente.

Meanwhile heat the oil in a large pan over a medium heat and sauté the shallots and garlic for 3–4 minutes, over a low to medium heat, until softened.

Pour in the wine and bring to the boil. Stir in the brown crab meat, followed by the cream and reduce the heat to a gentle simmer. Add the white crab meat, red and green chilli, lemon zest and juice and parsley. Season well and stir everything together.

Lift the pasta out of the pan using tongs and into the sauce. Mix thoroughly and spoon into individual warmed bowls.

BBQ SCALLOPS WITH BLACK PUDDING, APPLE & HAZELNUT BUTTER

The Orkney Islands are a must to visit – they turned out to be my favourite place on the trip and it happened to be on day one. From the air, as you fly over, the coastline and beaches resemble those of the Caribbean with clear sand and turquoise waters. They provide the ideal habitat for some of the greatest seafood found in Britain. Together with the scenery from its Viking past, the historic stones and old fishing ports still looking as they have always done, this is a unique place. I cooked this dish on the harbour wall at Stromness, a lovely small fishing port.

SERVES 6

200g salted butter, softened
1 English apple, thinly sliced
   and diced
small bunch of flat-leaf
   parsley, chopped
small bunch of dill, chopped
100g hazelnuts, chopped
50g black pudding, skinned
   and chopped
sea salt and freshly ground
   black pepper
12 scallops with roes attached

To serve
crusty bread

You will need
6 scallop shells, cleaned
300g seaweed to sit the
   shells on (optional)

Light your BBQ. When the coals are silvery in colour, it's ready to cook on. There's no need to put the rack on top as the scallop shells are going to sit on top of the coals.

Put the butter into a large bowl and add the apple, herbs, hazelnuts and black pudding. Season and mix well.

Pop 2 scallops in each shell, season, then spoon a sixth of the butter mixture on top of each one.

Place the shells directly onto the BBQ coals and cook for 3 minutes until the butter is hot and bubbling. Use long tongs to carefully lift each shell off the hot coals.

Divide the seaweed between six plates, if using, and sit a scallop shell on top of each pile. Serve with plenty of crusty bread to mop up the sauce. (Pictured overleaf.)

BACON, SCALLOPS & APPLES WITH ONION RINGS

Northern Ireland's golf courses are renowned as some of the best in the world but are an odd place to cook, even if you have the famous Belfast shipyard behind you. I toasted the oats in the bacon fat, as Paul Rankin said I should, and it worked, as did the amazing black butter we found in shops here. Made from cider apples, it's also made on Jersey and you can buy it online. It's great with cheese but delicious in this dish with the toasted oats.

SERVES 4

1 tablespoon olive oil
15g salted butter
8 thick slices of streaky bacon
8 scallops, cleaned, roes removed
sea salt and freshly ground
    black pepper
50g black butter (or 25g salted
    butter and 25ml black treacle
    mixed together)
50g rolled oats
100ml veal jus
50ml dry cider
100ml jar of apple sauce,
    blitzed until smooth

For the onion rings
1 litre vegetable oil,
    for deep-frying
50ml whole milk
25g plain flour
1 large shallot, cut into
    thin rings

Heat a large frying pan over a medium heat until hot. Add the oil and butter and fry the bacon and scallops for 1–2 minutes, seasoning as they cook and tossing every now and then, until crisp and golden. Pop onto a large plate and keep warm.

Put the pan back on the heat and add the black butter and oats. Stir together, season and cook for 1–2 minutes, then top the bacon slices with this mixture.

Put the same pan back on the heat again and pour in the veal jus and cider. Simmer for a few minutes over a high heat until reduced by half. Set the sauce aside and keep warm.

Now for the onion rings: heat the vegetable oil to 160°C (325°F) in a deep, heavy-based saucepan, or until a breadcrumb sizzles and turns brown when dropped into it. (Note: hot oil can be dangerous; do not leave unattended.) Line a plate with kitchen paper.

Put the milk and flour into two separate bowls and season the flour. Dip the shallot rings into the milk, then into the flour and toss to coat. Carefully lower into the oil and fry for 1–2 minutes, until golden and crisp. Lift out and drain on the kitchen paper and season with a pinch of salt.

Spoon the apple sauce into a piping bag and pipe onto 4 plates, top each with 2 scallops and 2 oat-topped slices of bacon and finish with a few onion rings. Drizzle over the sauce and serve.

PRAWN & LIME FLATBREADS

Grace Dent, the brilliant food critic, and I were on a narrow boat in Birmingham, as you do, looking at the sights. Birmingham has a strong, diverse community and fantastic produce which makes it a food destination to explore – the way the city is evolving, building and moving forward fascinates me, and the food scene here is doing the same. These flatbreads are a fantastic combination of flavours inspired by this great city.

SERVES 2

150–175ml warm water
3g fast-action dried yeast
325g plain flour, plus extra
 for dusting
a pinch of sea salt
60ml natural yogurt

For the topping
300g raw tiger prawns,
 peeled and de-veined
1 teaspoon mild chilli powder
1½ teaspoons garam masala
1 teaspoon curry powder
1 teaspoon nigella seeds
1 red onion, finely sliced
a generous pinch of sea salt
1 tablespoon olive oil
zest and juice of 1 lime
4 tablespoons lime
 pickle, chopped

To serve
4 tablespoons natural yogurt
small handful of mint,
 roughly chopped
small handful of coriander,
 roughly chopped
1–2 tablespoons chopped
 pistachios

Measure the water in a jug and stir in the yeast until it's dissolved. Stir the flour and salt together in a large bowl. Add the yogurt, followed by the yeasted warm water. Stir everything together then tip onto a clean work surface and knead for 5 minutes until smooth. The dough should be sticky, but not impossible to work with. Shape the dough into a ball then drop it into a clean bowl, cover with a clean tea towel and leave to rise in a warm place for about 1 hour.

Preheat the oven to 220°C (200°C fan)/425°F/gas 7 and slide 2 baking sheets (or use a pizza stone if you have one) in to preheat.

Just before the dough is ready, prepare the topping. In a bowl, mix the prawns with the chilli powder, garam masala, curry powder, nigella seeds and onion, then season with a good pinch of salt and drizzle over the olive oil. Finally stir in the lime zest and juice and toss everything together.

When the dough has risen, knock it back on a clean work surface dusted with a little flour. Divide into 2 pieces, then dust the work surface again generously with flour. Take one piece and roll it into a round, shaping as you roll, until it measures around 20cm in diameter.

Spread the dough with half of the lime pickle and top with half of the prawn and onion mix. Do the same again with the remaining dough, pickle and prawn mixture.

Carefully slide each flatbread onto the preheated baking sheets or pizza stone and bake for about 15 minutes, or until the bread has puffed up and is fully cooked through. The prawns should also be completely cooked (they should be pink and curled into a C-shape).

To serve, slide the flatbreads onto a board and slice into pieces. Add dollops of the yogurt and sprinkle with the chopped mint and coriander and the chopped pistachios.

LANGOUSTINES AT THE HARBOUR

Strangford Lough produces the best langoustines I have ever had, so much so that this was first on the list of places I wanted to visit. Situated a few miles south east of Belfast, this is the largest inlet in the British Isles and is linked to the sea by a narrow channel that brings in the rich waters that make it the perfect place to find the best seafood around. Great fish are caught here too – whiting, ray and haddock are some of the many species that come from this very special place.

SERVES 6

400g Comber (or other early
   new) potatoes, unpeeled
24 large raw langoustines
4 spring onions, sliced
small bunch of dill, chopped
1 lemon, cut into wedges

For the mayonnaise
3 egg yolks
1 tablespoon Dijon mustard
1 teaspoon white wine vinegar
200ml vegetable oil
sea salt and freshly ground
   black pepper
juice of 1 lemon

Bring a large pan of water to the boil and cook the potatoes for around 15 minutes, until tender. Drain well then tip into a bowl and chop roughly, then set aside to cool completely.

Bring another large pan of water to the boil and cook 18 of the langoustines for 1 minute. Drain well.

Heat a large griddle pan over a medium heat until hot. Put the remaining 6 langoustines on a board. Hold the body of one with your finger and thumb and, with the blade of a large chopping knife pointing towards the tail, push the point of the knife into the lateral line in the middle then slice down the body towards the tail to cut quickly and evenly through the shell and the flesh. Turn the langoustine round and slice through the head to make 2 halves. Pull out and remove the vein (a thin black strip) from each side and pull out the gut from the head – it should lift out in one piece.

Repeat with the other 5 langoustines then cook the halved langoustines on the griddle, shell-side down first, for around 3 minutes on each side, until charred and the flesh is opaque.

To make the mayonnaise, whisk the egg yolks, mustard and vinegar together in a medium bowl until smooth. Slowly pour the vegetable oil into the bowl, starting with a little drizzle and whisking well. This is easiest to do with an electric hand whisk. Continue to drizzle in the remaining oil, whisking all the time, until the mixture has thickened. Season to taste.

Spoon half the mayonnaise into the bowl of potatoes. Add the spring onions and dill, season and mix everything together.

Stir the lemon juice into the remaining mayonnaise.

Take a large platter and spoon the langoustines into a pile, topping with the griddled langoustines. Spoon the potato salad on the side, followed by the mayonnaise. Serve with the lemon wedges.

SEAFOOD RISOTTO

Fishing off the Isle of Wight Needles was my first real go at sea fishing and it didn't disappoint. We used mackerel as bait and drifted over the drops and wrecks around the famous rocks and I caught a few bass. The taste of a fresh line-caught bass is a true delight and it goes brilliantly with the shellfish in this rich risotto.

SERVES 4

50g butter
1 garlic bulb, halved
small bunch of flat-leaf parsley,
    leaves separated and stalks
    roughly chopped
100ml dry white wine
500g mussels, cleaned and
    debearded (see my tip
    on page 82)
500g clams, cleaned
1 garlic clove, chopped
1 shallot, diced
200g risotto rice
250ml chicken stock
sea salt and freshly ground
    black pepper
4 x 200-g sea bass portions
25g samphire
50g mascarpone
25g parmesan, grated
2 tomatoes, skinned, deseeded
    and roughly chopped
100g white crab meat
juice of 1 lemon

Add a knob of the butter to a large saucepan and heat until it has melted. Stir in the garlic bulb halves and chopped parsley stalks, cook for 1 minute, then pour in half of the wine.

Pop the mussels and clams into the pan, cover with a lid and cook for 2–3 minutes, then use a slotted spoon to scoop them out of the pan and onto a plate. Pour the cooking liquor into a bowl, discard the parsley and garlic and set the pan aside. Remove the meat from the mussels and clams.

Put the same pan back over a medium heat and add another knob of the butter. When it's melted, add the chopped garlic, shallot, rice, the remaining wine and three-quarters of the stock. Bring this to the boil then allow it to simmer for 15 minutes, stirring occasionally. Add the cooking liquor from the clams and mussels, leaving the last bit as it may contain sediment.

Pop a non-stick frying pan on the hob, season the bass and add the remaining butter to the pan. Place the fish into the pan skin-side down and hold it down with a fish slice for a minute to stop it from curling up. Cook for 2 minutes then flip over and add the samphire to the pan. Continue to cook for another 2 minutes.

To finish the risotto, add the clam and mussel meat to the rice mixture, followed by the mascarpone, parmesan, tomatoes, crab meat, lemon juice and the remaining stock. Stir everything together and check the seasoning. The texture should be slightly runny – if it isn't, add a little hot water until it reaches the right consistency.

To serve, spoon the risotto onto plates, top with a piece of sea bass and arrange the samphire over the fish. (Pictured overleaf.)

LYMPSTONE MUSSELS

I have never seen anything like the contraption used by the mussel men of the River Exe. They don't use dredges, which wreck the sea bed; they use a self-flushing elevator that kind of hoovers up the mussels, causing less disturbance and producing a more sustainable supply all year round. The mussels are then cleaned, graded and put in purification tanks for a few days before being sold. Myles is the brains behind The Exmouth Mussel Company, so next time you're down there, pop in and say hi. It was a pleasure to cook these wonderful mussels with my mate Michael Caines.

SERVES 4

50g butter
100g smoked streaky bacon, chopped into lardons
1 onion, diced
2 celery sticks, diced
2 garlic cloves, crushed
sea salt and freshly ground black pepper
small bunch of sea aster
250ml cider
250ml double cream
2kg mussels, cleaned and debearded (see my tip on page 82)
4 thick slices of white crusty bread
2 tablespoons olive oil
small bunch of flat-leaf parsley, chopped

Heat a large casserole dish over a medium heat for a few minutes until hot, then add half the butter. When it has melted and is sizzling, add the bacon pieces and fry until crisp.

Add the diced onion and celery and the garlic and season well. Stir everything together and cook over a low heat for a few minutes, stirring every now and then.

Add the sea aster and pour in the cider and cream, then season with black pepper. Stir everything together then add the remaining butter. Once the butter has melted and the liquid is simmering, pop the mussels in and stir everything together. Cover the pan with a lid and cook for 4 minutes.

Drizzle the slices of bread with the olive oil and toast in a flat frying pan until charred. Check all the mussels have opened, discarding any that haven't, then tip into a serving bowl. Sprinkle over the parsley and serve with the toasted bread.

POULTRY
& GAME

WHISKY CHICKEN WITH WILD MUSHROOM & MUSTARD SAUCE

Edradour Distillery is one place I had to go back to on this trip, not just because it's beautiful but also because I wanted to check up on my barrel of whisky that is signed and maturing nicely. Set up in 1825, the distillery is hidden in a small valley in Perthshire and is Scotland's smallest traditional whisky distillery. This place is a picture, as is the owner Andrew – he is on hand most days making the spirit and leading tours and tastings. Use any single-malt whisky to add a delicious warmth to this dish.

SERVES 6

25g butter
1 x 2-kg chicken, jointed
    into 8 portions
sea salt and freshly ground
    black pepper
2 shallots, diced
1 garlic clove, chopped
50ml whisky
1 tablespoon Dijon mustard
1 tablespoon grainy mustard
200g new potatoes, halved
100g wild mushrooms
4 medium tomatoes, quartered
750ml chicken stock
75ml double cream
small bunch of flat-leaf
    parsley, chopped
small bunch of wild garlic, plus
    wild garlic flowers to serve

Heat a large, wide, non-stick sauté pan over a medium heat until hot. Add the butter and heat until melted, then add the chicken pieces, skin-side down. Season them all, then fry for about 10 minutes, until deep golden. Stir in the shallots and garlic and cook for 3–4 minutes, until starting to soften. Turn the chicken over so it's skin-side up.

Pour the whisky into the pan and bring to a bubble to burn off the alcohol. Stir in both types of mustard, then add the potatoes, mushrooms and tomatoes. Season well then stir in the stock, cover and bring to the boil. Reduce the heat and simmer gently for 20 minutes, or until the chicken is cooked through. Cut through the thickest piece of meat and check there are no pink juices.

When the chicken is cooked, pour over the double cream and stir in the parsley. Add the wild garlic to the pan and cook for around 1 minute until it's wilted, then remove from the heat, sprinkle the flowers over the top and serve.

CHICKEN KIEV WITH WILD GARLIC & CREAMED WELSH LEEKS

You don't have to use wild garlic for this dish, but when it's in season it is one of the joys of foraged food. Not to be mistaken for lily of the valley, which is poisonous, you can often smell this plant in woodlands or along pathways and roads before you see it – Britain seems to provide the perfect growing conditions. I cooked this in Wales after driving the Llangollen Railway steam train the 10 miles to Corwen. It's a volunteer-run railway and a visit there is like stepping back in time.

SERVES 2

1–2 litres vegetable oil, for deep-frying
200g butter
7 garlic cloves, chopped
small bunch of wild garlic, chopped
small bunch of flat-leaf parsley, chopped
sea salt and freshly ground black pepper
2 x 150-g French-trimmed chicken breasts (ask your butcher to do this or use regular chicken breasts)
2 eggs, beaten
75g plain flour
100g panko breadcrumbs
400g Welsh leeks, washed, cut into 8-cm lengths and halved lengthways
100ml double cream
juice of ½ lemon

Heat the vegetable oil in a deep-fat fryer to 165–170°C (330–340°F) or in a deep, heavy-based saucepan until a breadcrumb sizzles and turns brown when dropped into it. (Note: hot oil can be dangerous; do not leave unattended.) Line a large plate with kitchen towel.

Put the butter, garlic, half the wild garlic and half the parsley into a bowl. Season and mix well.

Pull off the skin from each chicken breast and discard then carefully pull away the fillet. Cut a hole all the way through the chicken breast from the top almost to the bottom to create a pocket. Fill each with half the flavoured butter then push the chicken fillet into the chicken breast to fill the hole.

Put the beaten eggs in one shallow bowl, the flour in another and the breadcrumbs in another. Season the flour well. Coat each chicken breast first in flour, then in egg, and then again so they're coated with each twice. Next, coat with the breadcrumbs, pressing these into the skin so the chicken is completely covered.

Carefully lower the chicken pieces into the hot oil and fry for 10–12 minutes, until golden brown and cooked through. To test if the chicken is cooked, pierce the thickest part with a skewer to check the juices run clear. Lift onto the kitchen paper and season with salt.

Meanwhile, dry-fry the leeks in a frying pan over a medium heat for 2–3 minutes, stirring to keep them moving, until they're nicely charred. Pour the cream into the pan along with the remaining parsley and wild garlic. Season and stir everything together. Continue to cook for 3–4 minutes until softened and cooked down. Taste to check the seasoning then stir in the lemon juice.

To serve, spoon the leeks onto two warmed plates and pop a chicken Kiev alongside.

CHICKEN BALTI

Birmingham is the home of the balti and was the perfect place to visit with the food critic Grace Dent. We wanted to explore what this great city has to offer and, trust me, it offers a lot. It has more Michelin-starred restaurants than any other British city outside London and a buzzing food scene. While we were here, we had to cook a balti. It is said to have originated in north Pakistan and became popular in Birmingham in the early 1970s when we all lapped it up, just as the crew did shortly after I cooked this.

SERVES 4

4 skinless, boneless chicken breasts, chopped into 3-cm pieces
2 garlic cloves, crushed with 1 teaspoon salt
4-cm piece fresh ginger, grated
1½ teaspoons mild chilli powder
2 teaspoons garam masala
juice of 1 lemon

For the sauce
2 tablespoons olive oil
1 red onion, finely diced
2 cinnamon sticks
2 bay leaves
5 cardamom pods, lightly crushed
2 teaspoons mild chilli powder
4 teaspoons garam masala
3 tablespoons fresh fenugreek leaves, finely chopped (or 1 tablespoon dried)
sea salt and freshly ground black pepper
400-g can chopped tomatoes
1 large fresh tomato, roughly chopped into 2-cm chunks
2 teaspoons light soft brown sugar
75ml double cream
small bunch of coriander, chopped

To serve
naan bread, warmed according to packet instructions

First marinate the chicken – put the chicken pieces in a sealable container and add the garlic, ginger, chilli powder, garam masala and lemon juice. Stir everything together, cover and chill for up to 2 hours. If you're pushed for time, you can marinate it for just 15 minutes. When the chicken has finished marinating, take it out of the fridge to come to room temperature.

To make the sauce, heat the oil in a large pan over a medium to high heat and when hot, add the diced onion. Cook for about 8 minutes over a medium heat, stirring all the time, until the onion has softened and is lightly coloured.

Add the cinnamon sticks, bay leaves and cardamom pods and continue to fry for 1 minute, stirring everything around. Add the chilli powder, garam masala and fenugreek leaves and stir-fry again for a further minute.

Increase the heat and add the marinated chicken and season with a good pinch of salt. Stir the chicken into the onion and spices and fry for about 5 minutes, until starting to colour, then add all the tomatoes. Stir everything together, season, bring up to a simmer and cook for 20 minutes.

The chicken should now be cooked through but check by slicing a big piece in half; there should be no pink meat. Reduce the heat right down to low, then stir in the sugar, double cream and coriander and cook for 1–2 minutes to heat through. Taste to check the seasoning then serve with the warmed naan.

CHICKEN VERONIQUE

Camel Valley Vineyard is one of many success stories on the British wine scene. Bob and Annie Lindo bought this place originally to farm animals but soon realised the soil's potential for growing vines. They planted some to try and have gone on to produce world-leading fizz and wine with many awards to prove it. They make one of the best British sparkling wines I've tasted and it's well worth a visit to fill the boot with some of their finest. This dish is traditionally made with fresh sole but I loved the idea of a white chicken stew, and this is a great way to add good wine and grapes to make a tasty and special dish.

SERVES 4

1 x 2-kg corn-fed chicken
1 celery stick, sliced
1 medium onion, peeled
    and sliced
1 medium leek, sliced
5 black peppercorns
a few sprigs of thyme
2 bay leaves
1 garlic clove, sliced
50g butter
25g plain flour
100ml white wine
150ml double cream
sea salt and freshly ground
    black pepper
200g white grapes
    (peeled, optional)
a few sprigs of tarragon,
    leaves picked

Put the chicken on a board with the neck end facing towards you and snip off any string holding the chicken together. Lift up the flap of skin around the neck and use a small sharp knife to cut away and remove the wishbone, working as close to the bone as possible.

Take a chopping knife and cut the legs and thighs off each side and pull off the skin, then put them to one side. Working from the backbone, cut down one side to carefully remove one of the breasts, keeping the wing attached at the bottom. Do the same on the other side. Pull the skin off the chicken breasts and discard. Cut through the joint halfway through the wing to remove the tip, then slice from the top down, around the bone to remove the skin and flesh from the bone. Slice a thin piece off each knuckle so that the bone stands up.

Pop the chicken pieces into a large non-stick pan and pour enough cold water in to cover the joints. (You can save the bits of chicken that you're not using to make a stock – wrap up, label and freeze for up to 3 months.) Add the celery, onion, leek, peppercorns, thyme, bay leaves and garlic. Cover and place over a medium heat and bring to the boil. Reduce the heat slightly and simmer for 20 minutes to poach the chicken until it's cooked through.

Lift the chicken out of the pan onto a warm plate. Strain the stock into a bowl and discard the vegetables, herbs and spices.

Set the pan back on the hob over a low to medium heat and add half of the butter. Once it has melted and is foaming, whisk in the flour and cook for a minute, then whisk in the wine, 300ml of the reserved stock and the cream. Simmer for a few minutes until the sauce is smooth. Add the remaining butter and allow to melt, then whisk this in to finish the sauce. Season.

Add the chicken to the sauce and simmer for a minute or two to heat through, then stir in the grapes and sprinkle over the tarragon and serve.

ROAST DUCK IN HAY & LAVENDER

Cooking in hay is not a new technique and is a method that adds a great earthy flavour to duck, game and even chicken. The use of lavender adds even more flavour but there are thousands of types out there, so make sure you choose a light culinary English lavender (*Lavandula angustifolia*) for cooking otherwise it can taste of Gran's soap.

SERVES 3

3 large (approx. 225g) duck
　　breasts
sea salt and freshly ground
　　black pepper
3 handfuls of hay
6 sprigs of lavender
2 tablespoons lavender honey
2 carrots, cut into batons
2 parsnips, cut into batons
25g butter
50ml red wine
300ml veal jus
1 teaspoon sherry vinegar
zest of 1 orange
100g Brussels sprouts,
　　separated into leaves

Preheat the oven to 200°C (180°C fan)/400°F/gas 6.

Heat a large frying pan over a medium heat until hot. Put the duck breasts on a board and season, then fry skin-side down for 3 minutes to render the fat, until the skin is golden.

Line an ovenproof dish or roasting tin with the hay and lavender, then sit the duck breasts on top, skin-side up. (Set the frying pan aside to use again.) Drizzle the duck with the honey and roast for 12–15 minutes. Cover with foil and set aside to rest.

If there is a lot of duck fat in the frying pan, you might want to pour a little out. Add the carrot and parsnip batons to the pan, along with a knob of the butter and cook over a medium heat for 5 minutes until golden, tossing every now and then. Cover to keep warm.

To make the sauce, pour the wine and veal jus into a medium saucepan and bring to the boil. Reduce the heat to a simmer and cook until reduced by half. Whisk in the remaining butter, the sherry vinegar and orange zest and season.

Add the sprout leaves to the frying pan and stir into the veg until they're wilted.

Transfer the duck to a board and carve each breast into 3. Stir any rested juices into the sauce. Spoon the vegetables onto a warm platter, arrange the duck on top, drizzle the sauce over and serve.

SPICED PIGEON BREAST WITH DHAL

A London rooftop was the filming location for this on one of the hottest days of the year. I'd been driving the smallest car with no aircon around the busy streets. I didn't mind, to be honest, as it was a trip down memory lane for me visiting all the old sites where I used to work as a young cook: Harvey's, Nico's, Alastair Little and La Tante Claire. London is now awash with the best restaurants and hotels in the world – Bosi, John Williams, Clare Smyth, Chavot – there are so many, it is hard to choose a dish that sums up London now. I played safe and went for one we used to make at the bistro I worked at 30 years ago. This is simple and tasty and I remember it like it was yesterday. The thing is it isn't, and it takes me longer to make now I'm older!

SERVES 4

3 tablespoons natural yogurt
1½ teaspoons turmeric
1 garlic clove, crushed
zest and juice of 1 lemon
8 wood pigeon breasts, skin on
1 tablespoon olive oil

For the dhal
80g butter
1 onion, diced
5-cm piece fresh ginger, chopped
3 garlic cloves, chopped
2 teaspoons black mustard seeds
1½ teaspoons turmeric
2 teaspoons ground coriander
2 teaspoons garam masala
sea salt and freshly ground
    black pepper
250g yellow split peas,
    soaked overnight in cold
    water and drained
small bunch of coriander,
    roughly chopped
small bunch of mint, leaves
    picked and roughly chopped

To serve
seeds from ½ pomegranate

First marinate the pigeon. Put the yogurt, turmeric, garlic, lemon zest and juice into a sealable bag and squish it all together to mix. Add the pigeon breasts, seal the bag then massage to mix the marinade into the pigeon. Chill in the fridge and leave to marinate for a couple of hours or preferably overnight.

When you're ready to cook, start with the dhal. Melt half the butter in a large saucepan over a medium heat. Add the onion and fry, stirring regularly, for about 10 minutes, until soft and golden.

Stir in the ginger and garlic and fry for another minute, then add the mustard seeds, turmeric, coriander and garam masala. Season well and cook the spices for 1–2 minutes, then add the split peas and 750ml water. Bring to the boil then reduce the heat to a simmer, cover with a lid and cook the split peas for around 40 minutes until tender. You may have to add a little more water depending on how large your pan is.

When the dhal is cooked, remove the pigeon from the fridge. Remove the breasts from the bag and drizzle with the oil. Preheat a griddle pan over a medium heat until hot, then cook the pigeon for 2 minutes on each side, until charred. The flesh will feel firm and be pink in the middle. Lift onto a warm plate, cover and leave to rest for 2 minutes.

While the pigeon is resting take the cooked dhal off the heat and stir through the remaining butter and most of the chopped coriander and mint.

Spoon the dhal into warmed bowls, place a couple of pigeon breasts on top of each and sprinkle with the pomegranate seeds and the remaining herbs.

PARTRIDGE WITH VEGETABLES & SLOE GIN SAUCE

Cooking game in season outdoors was one of the joys of filming on this trip – I cooked this dish by the River Test in Laverstoke and I can think of no better place to make something like this. The British game season kicks off on 12th August with grouse and runs through until the end of January, with pheasant and partridge from October onwards. Partridge is one of the cheapest sources of protein – I've seen butchers selling them for less than £1 each. Cooked simply with seasonal ingredients, they won't disappoint.

SERVES 2

25ml olive oil
100g bacon lardons
50g baby onions
sea salt and freshly ground black pepper
2 spatchcocked partridges (see my tip below)
500ml hot beef stock
50ml sloe gin
25g butter
4 large Jerusalem artichokes, sliced
100g whole wild mushrooms
50g rainbow chard, chopped and tough stalks removed
2 tablespoons quince jelly

Heat the oil in a large, non-stick frying pan and fry the bacon and onions for 5 minutes, until the onions have started to soften and the bacon has started to turn golden. Push them to one side of the pan.

Season the partridges on both sides then place them in the pan, skin-side down, and cook for 2 minutes. Turn them over and cook for a further 2–3 minutes. Pour in the stock and sloe gin, season, bring to the boil and simmer for 8–10 minutes so that the partridges cook and the sauce reduces.

In a separate medium saucepan, melt the butter over a medium heat and when it is foaming, stir in the artichokes. Cook, stirring often, for 3–4 minutes, then add the mushrooms and chard. Season well and cook for a further 2 minutes, stirring everything together.

Take the partridge out of the sauce and transfer to a board to rest. Increase the heat a little under the frying pan to bring the sauce to the boil, then simmer until it's reduced by a third.

Carve the legs off each partridge then carve down either side of the breast bones to remove the breasts. The meat should be nice and pink in the middle. Divide the artichoke mixture between two warm plates and place the pieces of partridge on top. Drizzle over the sauce, spoon the onions and bacon on top and dot with quince jelly.

JAMES'S TIP

You can ask your butcher to spatchcock the partridges for you, but if you want to do it yourself here's how. Put the birds on a board, breast-side down. Take a sharp pair of kitchen scissors and cut down both sides of the backbone and remove it. Open the bird out, then turn it over and use the heel of your hand to press down on the breastbone to flatten it. Push a skewer diagonally through from the top of the breast on one side to the drumstick on the other. Repeat on the other side.

GUINEA FOWL WITH BRAMBLES

Michael Caines's garden at his amazing hotel on the banks of the River Exe was the location for this cook. Well, it used to be a garden but the man is Michael Caines, the genius chef, and things move quickly here and he's planted 10 acres of beautiful vines since my last visit only a few months before! I love his vision and drive; it's infectious and you can tell it's driving his team, too, as this inspiring place starts to take shape. Guinea fowl are native to Africa, but they're now farmed throughout Britain and make a great choice for people wanting to try game. About the size of a medium chicken, they have a stronger flavour and will stand up to robust ingredients like wild brambles. In Devon in September there were shed loads of them.

SERVES 4

100g bacon, cut into lardons
1 tablespoon plain flour
sea salt and freshly ground
    black pepper
1 guinea fowl, jointed into
    8 pieces
1 medium carrot, diced
1 medium leek, diced
1 shallot, diced
500ml chicken stock
50ml double cream
1 tablespoon runny honey
small bunch of tarragon
200g brambles/blackberries

Heat a large non-stick casserole over a medium heat for a few minutes until hot. Add the bacon and fry until crispy.

Sprinkle the flour onto a plate and season well. Toss the guinea fowl pieces in the flour to coat, then cook them in batches, frying each piece until golden brown. Lift onto a plate and set aside.

Add the carrot, leek and shallot to the pan and stir together, then return the guinea fowl to the pan and pour in the stock. Bring to the boil, pop a lid on, then reduce the heat to a simmer and cook for 20–25 minutes.

Stir the cream into the sauce, followed by the honey and season to taste. Spoon into warmed bowls and sprinkle over the tarragon and brambles. (Pictured overleaf.)

MEAT

BEEF WELLINGTON

The history of this dish is unclear. Some say it's named after the Duke of Wellington's love of these ingredients and after his boot. Others say it comes from New Zealand. Either way, the combination of pâté, mushrooms and pastry wrapped around a fillet of beef is a true classic. The pancakes are important as they help soak up the juices from the beef and stop the pastry becoming soggy.

SERVES 6

vegetable oil, for frying
sea salt and freshly ground
    black pepper
600g beef fillet, cut from
    the centre
400g chestnut mushrooms,
    roughly chopped
25g salted butter
100g spinach
500g ready-made puff pastry
plain flour, for rolling out
100g chicken liver pâté
2 egg yolks, beaten

For the pancakes
100g plain flour
2 eggs
300ml milk

For the sauce
500ml veal jus
100ml Madeira
25ml red wine
15g salted butter

Preheat the oven to 200°C (180°C fan)/400°F/gas 6.

Place a medium frying pan over a medium heat until hot. Drizzle with a little oil. Season the beef and pan-fry quickly all over to seal. Lift into a roasting tin and roast for 20 minutes. Take the beef out of the oven, lift onto a plate to cool and chill until you're ready to assemble the dish. Reserve the meat juices. Leave the oven on.

Whizz the mushrooms in a food processor until finely chopped. Melt half the butter in a medium saucepan and add the mushrooms. Season well, stir in the beef juices and cook until softened. Tip into a bowl and wipe out the pan. Melt the remaining butter in the pan, add the spinach and season. Sauté until the spinach is just wilted, then squeeze out all the liquid and spoon onto a tray lined with a clean tea towel to drain.

Whisk all the pancake ingredients together in a bowl. Heat a medium frying pan until hot and drizzle in a little oil. Wipe round with kitchen paper so it's very lightly oiled. Spoon a ladleful of batter into the pan, swirl around until it covers the base and cook until just set. Flip over and cook on the other side for 30 seconds. Transfer to a plate and cover with greaseproof paper. Continue to make pancakes until you've used up all the batter and leave them to cool.

Roll out the puff pastry on a lightly floured surface into a rectangle measuring 40 x 20cm, about 2mm thick. Arrange the pancakes on top of the pastry and spread the pâté evenly over the pancakes, leaving a 2-cm gap along the top and bottom edges, then season. Next, spread out the mushrooms and spinach. Put the beef in the centre and season. Brush the edges of the pastry with the beaten egg, fold them over and roll it all over. Egg-wash again and use a table knife swirl to decorate, but don't cut through the pastry. Carefully lift onto a baking sheet and bake for 20 minutes.

Meanwhile, pour the veal jus, Madeira and red wine into a medium pan and simmer until reduced by half. Add the butter, season and whisk together to finish the sauce.

Slice the beef into 6 portions and spoon over the sauce.

ONE-POT BEEF STEW & DUMPLINGS

Castle Howard is home to Aberdeen Angus cattle, grazing around the Temple of the Four Winds and the Mausoleum, which both sit in the estate. Mike Fargher farms his beef on the lush pasture all around here – a stone's throw from where our farm used to be. His meat is sold in the local shop at the castle and you have to try it if you visit. This is a classic beef recipe to showcase a beautiful ingredient.

SERVES 4

2 tablespoons plain flour
sea salt and freshly ground
    black pepper
1kg beef shin, diced
1 tablespoon olive oil
2 onions, diced
2 garlic cloves, diced
1 bouquet garni (made from
    2 bay leaves and 2 thyme
    sprigs tied with kitchen string)
500ml beef stock

For the dumplings
200g self-raising flour,
    plus extra for dusting
125g suet
small bunch of flat-leaf
    parsley, chopped

Spoon the plain flour into a bowl and season well, then add the diced beef and toss to coat. Heat the oil in a large casserole pan over a medium heat and fry the beef in batches, until well browned, adding more oil if you need to. Transfer the beef to a bowl as you go.

Return the beef and any juices to the pan and add the onions, garlic and the bouquet garni. Stir everything together and pour over the stock. Cover with a lid and bring to the boil. Turn the heat down to a simmer and cook for 2 hours, or until the beef is very tender.

Preheat the oven to 200°C (180°C fan)/400°F/gas 6.

To make the dumplings, tip the flour into a large bowl. Stir in the suet and parsley and season well. Pour 150ml cold water over the top and stir everything together to make a rough dough. Divide the mixture into 10 or 12 portions. Dust your hands with flour and roll into balls.

Turn the heat off under the casserole. Take the lid off the pan and pop the balls on top of the stew, spacing them evenly apart. Place the casserole, uncovered, into the oven and cook for 30 minutes until the dumplings have plumped up and are cooked through.

ABERDEEN ANGUS SIRLOIN STEAK WITH WHISKY SAUCE

Aberdeen Angus beef is world-renowned for its quality. Mostly grass-fed, the cows produce meat that is full of flavour and so tender if you cook it well. The key to cooking with whisky is getting rid of the alcohol to leave you the great flavour, so flaming the whisky while cooking the dish is a must. The sauce also works with game and pork.

SERVES 2

1 tablespoon olive oil, plus extra for frying
400g Aberdeen Angus sirloin steak, at room temperature
sea salt and freshly ground black pepper
25g salted butter
4 shallots, halved through the root
small bunch of asparagus, halved
100g chestnut mushrooms, quartered
2 garlic cloves, crushed
50ml whisky
100ml double cream
a few tarragon sprigs, leaves picked

Place a griddle pan over a medium heat and heat until hot.

Rub the oil over each side of the steak and season well. Lay the steak on the griddle pan – it should sizzle when you put it in – and cook for 2 minutes. Turn the steak around 90 degrees and cook for a further 2–3 minutes, then flip it over again and cook for another 2 minutes.

Meanwhile, in a large, non-stick frying pan, melt the butter over a medium to high heat and add a drizzle of olive oil. Cook the shallots, cut-side down, until charred.

Add the asparagus and continue to cook over a high-ish heat for a few more minutes, then add the mushrooms to the pan. Stir everything around and continue to cook until all the vegetables are golden and charred.

Stir in the garlic and cook for about 1 minute, then pour in the whisky. Flambé to burn off the alcohol, then pour in the cream and add the tarragon. Season well and simmer for a couple of minutes until the sauce cooks and thickens slightly.

Lift the steak onto a board and let it rest for 5 minutes, then slice into 2-cm pieces.

To serve, spoon the vegetables and sauce onto a platter and top with the sliced steak. (Pictured overleaf.)

INDIVIDUAL BEEF PIES WITH OYSTERS

If you've never eaten the classic combination of beef and oysters, you should try it.
I made this in Cornwall where Paul Ainsworth and I got amazing oysters from Luke,
the oyster farmer at Porthilly. Run by the Marshall family for five generations, Porthilly
Farm sits in a prime position on the water surrounded by lush pasture on one side
with their cattle grazing and the multi-million-pound houses of Rock on the other.
The place is perfect for oyster production thanks to the tidal stream bringing
seawater to feed and filter the oysters.

SERVES 6

3 tablespoons vegetable oil
2kg shin of beef, diced
sea salt and freshly ground
    black pepper
2 shallots, peeled and diced
500ml beef stock
250ml British bitter
a little plain flour, for rolling out
500g ready-made puff pastry
2 egg yolks, for egg wash

For the oysters (optional)
large bunch of flat-leaf parsley
100g sourdough bread,
    roughly chopped
zest of 1 lemon
12 just-shucked oysters
    in their shells

You will need
6 x 12.5-cm pie dishes

Heat the oil in a very large, non-stick casserole pan then fry the
meat, in batches, until well browned all over. Transfer each batch
to a plate as you do it and season well.

Once all the meat has been browned, return it to the pan with the
shallots and pour over the stock and beer. Cover, bring to the boil
then reduce the heat and simmer gently for 2 hours. Spoon into a
large shallow dish and cool. You can make the stew up to a day in
advance and chill in the fridge until you want to assemble the pies.

Preheat the oven to 200°C (180°C fan)/400°F/gas 6.

Lightly dust a clean work surface with a little flour then roll out
the pastry until it is 2mm thick. Using the top of one of the pie dishes
as a guide, cut out 6 circles slightly larger than the dishes, then fill
the pie dishes with stew. (We used mini ovenproof saucepans.)

Brush the edges of the pastry lids with the egg wash then turn
over and lay on top of the dishes and seal around the edges. Brush
the tops with egg wash, sit the pies on a large baking tray and bake
for 40 minutes, until the pastry is crisp and golden.

While the pies are in the oven, prepare the oysters (if making).
Put the parsley and bread into a food processor and blitz to make
fine breadcrumbs. Add the lemon zest and blitz again. Season well.

Arrange the oysters on a baking tray, spoon the crumb mixture
over the top and bake on the top shelf of the oven for 10 minutes.

To serve, pop the pies onto plates with 2 oysters per person.

HERB-COATED BEEF WITH BEETROOTS & YORKSHIRE PUDDINGS

I love this dish not just because of the beef and beetroot (and of course the puddings), but for its simple flavours. Great beef and beetroot are perfect together and fresh beetroot taken straight from the ground into the pot tastes so much better than any flown halfway round the world in plastic bags.

SERVES 6

4 large beetroots
50g salted butter, softened
1kg fillet beef
1½ tablespoons treacle
small bunch of herbs (such as parsley and thyme), chopped

For the Yorkshire puddings
200g plain flour
sea salt and freshly ground black pepper
8 eggs
600ml whole milk
40g dripping

For the sauce
200ml red wine
400ml veal jus

You will need
a 12-hole large muffin tin

First make the Yorkshire pudding batter. Put the flour into a large bowl and season well. Mix together and make a well in the middle. Stir in the eggs, one at a time, then slowly pour in the milk, whisking continuously until the batter is smooth. Chill in the fridge for at least 30 minutes or for up to one day.

When you're ready to cook, preheat the oven to 220°C (200°C fan)/425°F/gas 7.

Put the beetroots into a medium pan and cover with cold water. Pop a lid on the pan and bring to the boil then reduce the heat and simmer for 40 minutes until the beetroots are tender. Lift them out of the pan and set aside to cool. Once cool, use kitchen paper to peel away the skins by wrapping them in the paper and rubbing. Cut each beetroot into quarters, trimming away the stalks. Beetroot juice stains hands for days so you may want to don a pair of rubber gloves while doing this.

To bake the Yorkshires, spoon 1 teaspoon of dripping into each of the muffin tin holes then heat it in the oven for 5 minutes until the dripping is hot. Carefully ladle the batter into each hole then bake for 30 minutes until the Yorkshires are well risen and browned.

To cook the beef, melt the butter in a large frying pan over a medium heat and fry the beef until browned all over. Season then brush the treacle all over and press the herbs onto the beef. Transfer the beef to a roasting tin, add the cooked beetroots and roast in the oven for 20 minutes for medium-rare.

Meanwhile, make the sauce. Pour the wine and veal jus into a pan and bring to the boil. Simmer until reduced by half, then pour into a serving jug.

Take the beef out of the oven and leave to rest for 10 minutes before slicing and serving with the Yorkshires, beetroots and sauce.

BEEF WITH CHAMP, CHARRED ONIONS & PARSLEY OIL

Champ is a traditional Irish dish of mash and spring onions; I've added cabbage here, so this is really a combination of champ and colcannon. I like to use big chunks of meat for this dish and cook it for slightly longer than usual. The braised onions add a nice rich touch to it.

SERVES 4

1 tablespoon vegetable oil
sea salt and freshly ground
    black pepper
4 x 150-g pieces beef shin
½ tablespoon plain flour
250ml red wine
4 whole onions, peeled
a few thyme sprigs
500ml beef stock

For the champ
25g butter
½ sweetheart cabbage,
    shredded
600g mashed potatoes
1 bunch of spring onions,
    chopped
100ml double cream

For the parsley oil
large bunch of flat-leaf
    parsley, leaves picked
100ml olive oil

Preheat the oven to 200°C (180°C fan)/400°F/gas 6.

Heat the oil in a large, lidded ovenproof pan or casserole until hot. Season the beef then brown each piece well on all sides. Turn the heat down if the oil starts to smoke. Lift out the meat and set aside.

Stir the flour into the pan and cook for 1 minute, then pour in the wine. Bring to the boil, then add the whole onions and thyme. Return the beef to the pan and pour the stock over the top. Cover the pan with the lid, bring to the boil, then transfer to the oven to cook for 2½ hours.

After 1 hour, lift the onions out with a slotted spoon, place in a shallow bowl and leave to cool. Continue to cook the beef for a further 1½ hours.

To make the champ, melt the butter in a large pan. Stir in the cabbage and cook for about 2 minutes, until wilted. Put the mash into a separate pan with the spring onions and cream. Heat over a low heat, stirring all the time until hot. Stir the cabbage into the mash and season. Cover and keep warm.

Carefully cut the whole onions in half horizontally. Heat a non-stick frying pan over a medium heat until hot. Pop the onions into the pan, cut-side down, and cook until charred.

To make the parsley oil, put the leaves and olive oil into a liquidiser, season and blitz for 2 minutes, until you have a bright green oil.

Divide the champ and beef between 4 warm plates, spoon the sauce over the top and drizzle with parsley oil. Place the onions on the side and serve.

50s BURGERS & SHAKES

Goodwood was the perfect place to cook this dish. The estate has amazing pasture and produces great lamb and beef, plus it holds one of the best events in Britain – the Goodwood Revival, celebrating all things from the 1950s and '60s in and around the race circuit. It's like stepping back in time with 200,000 plus visitors getting into the spirit and food harking back to when the Wimpy was the first burger brought to these shores. (If you go, make sure you dress up or you'll look like a muppet, trust me!)

SERVES 4

600g beef mince
sea salt and freshly ground
    black pepper
125-g ball buffalo mozzarella,
    quartered
a little oil, for frying
4 brioche buns, halved
1 large tomato, sliced
1 little gem lettuce, leaves
    separated
4 slices of Monterey Jack cheese
1 red onion, sliced

For the cucumber pickle
100ml white wine vinegar
50g caster sugar
1 teaspoon sea salt
3 baby cucumbers, sliced
    lengthways into 4

For the shakes
1 litre whole milk
375g raspberries, puréed
    in a blender

You will need
4 burger sticks

Start by making the pickle. Pour the vinegar into a large pan, add the sugar and salt and heat gently to dissolve them. You may need to stir the mixture every now and then. When they've dissolved, add the cucumber slices and remove the pan from the heat. Set aside to cool.

To make the burgers, put the mince into a bowl and season well. Mix together with your hands then divide into 4 even portions and shape each portion into a burger-shaped round. Push your thumb into the centre of one of them to make a hole (making sure you don't push all the way through) then fill with a piece of mozzarella. Cover the hole over with mince to seal it in. Do the same with the other burgers and remaining mozzarella.

Drizzle a large, flat griddle pan with oil. Place over a medium heat and when hot, lay the burgers in the pan. Reduce the heat and fry the burgers gently for 5 minutes. Flip them over and continue to cook them for a further 5 minutes.

Toast the brioche buns sliced-side down in the same pan.

To serve, place each brioche base onto a plate and top with slices of tomato and lettuce leaves, then a burger. Next add a slice of Monterey Jack cheese, some onion and slices of pickled cucumber. Pop the bun tops on and secure with a burger stick.

To make the shakes, whisk the milk and the raspberry purée together in a large jug or bowl. Pour into 4 glasses and serve alongside the burgers.

GRILLED VEAL CHOPS WITH BURRATA, TOMATOES & DEEP-FRIED COURGETTE FLOWERS

I saw these veal chops at the farm over on the Isle of Wight; they're a must whenever I see them in a butchers. In my mind, if you eat and drink milk you should eat veal, and we have some amazing veal now being produced in Britain. There is so much more to cooking with veal than just covering it in breadcrumbs and pan-frying it.

SERVES 2

2 veal chops
sea salt and freshly ground
    black pepper
1 tablespoon olive oil
1 garlic bulb, halved
6 medium tomatoes
a few sprigs of fresh basil
1–2 litres vegetable oil,
    for deep-frying
200g plain flour
200g sparkling water
8 courgette flowers
a few sprigs of oregano, leaves
    picked and chopped if large
1 tablespoon balsamic vinegar
1 burrata (approx. 125g)

Preheat the oven to 200°C (180°C fan)/400°F/gas 6.

Put the veal on a board and season all over. Heat an ovenproof frying pan over a medium heat until hot, then drizzle in half of the oil. Add the chops, followed by the garlic bulb and fry for 3–4 minutes until golden, then flip over and fry again for about 3–4 minutes on the other side. Add the whole tomatoes and basil, followed by the rest of the oil and transfer to the oven for 5 minutes.

Heat the vegetable oil in a deep-fat fryer to 180°C (350°F) or in a deep, heavy-based saucepan until a breadcrumb sizzles and turns brown when dropped into it. (Note: hot oil can be dangerous; do not leave unattended.) Line a large plate or tray with kitchen paper.

Whisk the flour and sparkling water together in a bowl to make a smooth batter, season with salt and whisk again. Dip the courgette flowers into the batter, making sure they're completely coated, then fry in the hot oil for 1–2 minutes or until golden. Lift out with a slotted spoon and drain on the kitchen paper, seasoning with salt straightaway.

Remove the veal chops from the oven and transfer them to a board. Cover and leave to rest. Put the pan back on the hob and season the pan's contents. Sprinkle in the oregano, drizzle in the balsamic vinegar and any rested juices from the board, and stir everything together to make a sauce.

To serve, pop a veal chop onto each plate, along with the tomatoes and garlic. Drizzle over the sauce, add the fried courgette flowers and sit half the burrata on top of each so it melts over.

CALVES LIVER WITH ONION GRAVY, CAVOLO NERO & MASH

I don't know what I was more excited about – the amazing plot of land full of stunning organic veg or the 1960s Massey Ferguson 135 tractor! It was the vehicle I learnt to drive on back on the farm, and the crew couldn't get me off it. Run by a small family in Devon, the plot where we made this dish supplies vegetables to nearby villages thereby giving the family an income and the villagers the best-tasting veg without the effort of growing it themselves. Cavolo nero, also known as 'Italian kale', is packed full of nutrients and goes brilliantly with liver.

SERVES 2

1 tablespoon vegetable oil
1 medium onion, thinly sliced
50ml Madeira
400ml veal jus
25g butter
1 teaspoon sherry vinegar
sea salt and freshly ground
    black pepper
4 x 100-g calves livers,
    thickly sliced
50g cavolo nero, chopped

For the mash
300g potatoes, peeled
    and chopped
50ml double cream
50g butter

Heat a medium saucepan over a medium heat and drizzle in the oil. Add the onion and sauté for around 5 minutes, stirring occasionally, until golden brown.

Pour the Madeira into the pan and flambé to burn off the alcohol, then add the jus and bring to the boil. Reduce the heat to a simmer and cook gently until reduced by half. Whisk in half of the butter and the sherry vinegar and season to taste. Cover to keep warm.

While the gravy is simmering, make the mash. Put the potatoes into a pan and cover with cold water. Add a pinch of salt, put a lid on, bring to the boil and simmer for around 15 minutes, until tender.

Heat a non-stick pan over a medium heat until hot then add the remaining butter. While the butter is melting, season the livers all over and when the butter begins to foam add the slices and cook on one side for 2 minutes. Flip them over and cook for another 2 minutes. Cover to keep warm.

When the potatoes are cooked, drain them well, pass through a ricer and return to the pan. Heat for a minute or so over a low heat to dry any moisture, add the double cream and butter, season and stir to combine. Cover to keep warm.

In a separate small saucepan, pour in 50ml water and bring to a simmer. Add the cavolo nero and cook for 2 minutes, until wilted, and season well.

To serve, spoon the mash between 2 plates followed by the cavolo nero. Top with slices of liver and finish by spooning over the onion gravy.

VENISON WITH BEETROOT & BLACKBERRIES

Blair Castle was the perfect place to explore the Scottish Highlands with the great chef Tom Kitchin. He really is a master of game cookery at his numerous restaurants in and around Edinburgh. He's also into his foraging so while he wandered off collecting from the woodland, I cooked this dish in the castle's stunning walled garden with former head keeper Sandy Reid. There is little he doesn't know about the place as he's been here since he was 15 as a pony boy. We talked about everything from food to the golden eagles and otters that live on this amazing estate. The roe deer venison he gave me to make this dish was probably the best I've ever tasted.

SERVES 4

3 x 200-g venison steaks
sea salt and freshly ground
    black pepper
1 tablespoon rapeseed oil
25g butter
½ small red cabbage,
    cut into 4 wedges
2 shallots, halved
2 large cooked beetroot,
    quartered
50g rainbow chard
1 small bunch of wild garlic

For the sauce
50ml red wine
1 tablespoon balsamic vinegar
100ml veal jus
1 tablespoon redcurrant jelly
3 juniper berries
2 star anise
10g butter

To serve
50g blackberries
a few wild garlic flowers
small handful of fennel fronds

Heat a large, non-stick frying pan over a medium heat until hot. Put the venison steaks on a board and season all over. Drizzle the oil into the pan and fry the venison on all sides – it will take around 2–3 minutes to cook it all over. Add the butter and, once it's melted, tip the pan to one side and spoon it over the venison. Cook for a further 4 minutes. Transfer the steaks to a warm plate, cover and leave to rest. Set the pan with the juices to one side.

Heat a large, flat griddle pan over a medium heat until hot, then pop the cabbage, shallots and beetroot on top and cook for 2–3 minutes on each side until tender and charred.

To make the sauce, pour the wine, vinegar and veal jus into the frying pan you cooked the venison in and bring to a simmer, scraping the bottom of the pan to deglaze it and stir in all the juices. Bring to the boil and add the redcurrant jelly, juniper berries and star anise, then reduce the heat and simmer for 3 minutes.

Put the chard and wild garlic onto the griddle and cook for a couple of minutes until wilted.

Remove the juniper berries and star anise from the sauce and discard, then add the butter and season.

To serve, pile the vegetables onto a platter, separating the shallots into layers. Slice the meat and arrange on top, adding any rested juices to the sauce. Warm the sauce through, then spoon over the meat and vegetables. Finally, scatter over the blackberries, wild garlic flowers and a few fennel fronds. (Pictured overleaf.)

VENISON WITH PARSNIPS THREE WAYS, RED WINE SAUCE & SWEETHEART CABBAGE

Parsnips are definitely one of my favourite vegetables – they are so versatile, as the name of this dish suggests. This recipe also works well with chicken, game and lamb, or you can use different veg and a vegetable stock instead of the veal jus to make a great vegetarian dish.

SERVES 4

4 large parsnips, peeled
  (peelings reserved)
250ml milk
3 small parsnips, unpeeled
25g butter
1 sweetheart cabbage,
  tough core removed
  and quartered
a few sprigs of rosemary
50g honey
50ml sherry
sea salt and freshly ground
  black pepper
2 x 300-g venison saddles
1 tablespoon olive oil
1–2 litres vegetable oil,
  for deep-frying

For the sauce
50ml sherry
50ml red wine
200ml veal jus
10g butter

Preheat the oven to 200°C (180°C fan)/400°F/gas 6.

Chop 3 of the large parsnips into a small dice, tip into a medium pan and pour over the milk. Cover, bring to the boil, then simmer for about 10 minutes or until the parsnips are soft.

Quarter the 3 small parsnips lengthways. Place an ovenproof frying pan over a medium heat and add 10g of the butter. As soon as the butter has melted, add the parsnips and fry until coloured, then add the cabbage and rosemary. Drizzle with the honey, then pour over the sherry and season well. Mix everything together then transfer to the oven to roast for 10–15 minutes.

Heat a non-stick frying pan over a medium heat until hot. Season the venison, then drizzle the oil into the pan and add the remaining butter. When the butter is foaming, add the venison to the pan and cook for 2–3 minutes, turning halfway through. Transfer to a roasting tin and roast for 4–5 minutes. Remove from the oven, cover and leave to rest for 4 minutes. Set aside the frying pan to make the sauce.

Heat the vegetable oil in a deep-fat fryer to 180°C (350°F) or in a deep, heavy-based saucepan until a breadcrumb sizzles and turns brown when dropped into it. (Note: hot oil can be dangerous; do not leave unattended.) Line a baking tray with kitchen paper.

Peel the remaining parsnip into ribbons and, together with the peelings from the other three large parsnips, deep-fry in batches for 2–3 minutes until golden. Use a slotted spoon to lift onto the kitchen paper and sprinkle with salt.

Heat the frying pan that the venison was cooked in over a medium heat. Pour in the sherry and wine and stir with a wooden spoon, scraping any bits off the base of the pan to deglaze it. Pour in the veal jus and bring to the boil, then simmer until reduced by half. Season and whisk in the butter.

Use a stick blender to whizz the diced parsnips and milk until you have a smooth purée, then season and put back on the heat to warm through.

Slice each piece of venison into 5 or 6 slices. Spoon the purée onto plates, add a few slices of venison, place a few roasted parsnips and a cabbage quarter alongside, spoon over the sauce and top with the parsnip crisps.

PORK CHOPS WITH BEANS, TOMATO & SALAMI STEW

The brilliant Lisa Goodwin-Allen from Northcote restaurant took me to see Holmes Mill in Clitheroe. It's the brain child of James Warburton and is quite impressive with a vast array of produce from near and far and experts on hand to show you what to do with it. It's the Harrods food hall of the North and is worth a trip to see it and to try a tipple of its home brew. I made this dish with the fantastic ingredients I found there.

SERVES 4

1 tablespoon olive oil
sea salt and freshly ground
    black pepper
4 pork chops
100g British salami, cut from a
    large sausage, then chopped
100g cherry tomatoes, halved
1 shallot, sliced
3 large garlic cloves, diced
100g padrón peppers
400-g can butter beans, drained
50g roasted red peppers, diced
50ml white wine
small bunch of curly parsley,
    chopped
15g butter

Heat a large frying pan until hot, then drizzle in the oil. Season the chops on both sides then pop in the pan and cook for 3–4 minutes on one side until golden. Turn them over and cook for a further 2–3 minutes.

Add the salami, tomatoes, sliced shallot and garlic and continue to cook for 3–4 minutes, stirring everything around, until the tomatoes have broken down slightly.

Next add the padrón peppers to the pan, along with the butter beans and roasted peppers. Mix all the ingredients together, pour in the wine and increase the heat to bring to the boil. Season, then sprinkle over the parsley and add the butter. Cook for a few more minutes until everything is heated through.

Spoon the vegetables onto a warm platter, arrange the chops on top and serve.

MIXED GRILL WITH PEPPERCORN SAUCE

This is a dish that's fallen out of favour over the years – I don't really know why – so when I visited Richard and Rosamund Vaughan and their rare breed animals at Huntsham Court Farm in the Wye Valley, I had to make a mixed grill. Their meat is some of the most delicious I've tasted and it takes this classic 1970s and '80s dish to another level. Don't just take my word for it – check out their website and see what great chefs around the country say about their produce. You can also order some of this amazing meat and find out for yourself.

SERVES 4–6

1 tablespoon olive oil
1 rump steak (approx. 250g)
4 lamb chops
sea salt and freshly ground
    black pepper
4 pork chops
6 pork sausages
2 pork kidneys
3 large vine tomatoes, halved

For the peppercorn sauce
30g butter
1 shallot, diced
1 garlic clove, sliced
a glug of brandy
300ml beef stock
1 tablespoon pink peppercorns
1 tablespoon green peppercorns
3 thyme sprigs
50ml double cream

Preheat the oven to 100°C (80°C fan)/210°F/gas ¼. Put a large platter in the oven to keep warm.

Put a large griddle pan over a high heat. Rub the oil over the rump steak and cook on the griddle for 4–6 minutes, turning halfway through. Depending on the thickness, this will cook the steak to medium rare. Add the lamb chops to the griddle and cook for 6–8 minutes, again turning halfway through. Season well, then transfer the meat to the platter in the oven to rest and keep warm.

Place the pork chops, sausages and kidneys onto the griddle. Turn the kidneys over after 3 minutes and continue to cook. Allow 6–8 minutes for the pork chops, turning halfway through, depending on their thickness. Turn the sausages regularly, allowing them to colour on all sides, and cook for 15–20 minutes, depending on how thick they are. Slice one in half to check it's cooked through.

Once the meat is cooked, remove it from the griddle, season well and set aside in the oven as before. Place the tomato halves, cut side down, onto the griddle, and cook for 1 minute on each side then transfer to the oven.

For the peppercorn sauce, place a high-sided frying pan over a medium heat. Add half the butter and as soon as it has melted, stir in the shallots. Cook over a low to medium heat for 3–4 minutes until starting to soften then stir in the garlic and cook for 1 minute.

Add a glug of brandy to the pan then flambé it to burn off the alcohol. Pour in the stock, then add both types of peppercorns (crush these a little beforehand if you wish) and the thyme and stir together. Boil rapidly until the sauce has reduced by half. Lower the heat and slowly add the cream, swirling the pan as you do, then stir in the remaining butter to make a smooth sauce. Season to taste and remove the thyme sprigs.

Take the platter of meat and tomatoes out of the oven, pour over the peppercorn sauce and serve.

FOREST PORK FEAST

Not only is Nottingham in a beautiful part of the country, it just happens to have a stunning restaurant and one of Britain's finest. Restaurant Sat Bains sits in an unusual site under a flyover and power lines just outside the city, but it has become a gastro hotspot thanks to the husband and wife team behind it. Brilliantly clever cooking makes for an amazing meal. After filming the whole day, I worked the evening service in the kitchen to see it at first hand, away from the cameras. How anyone can make beetroot and potatoes taste like that is beyond me, and if you think I was going to make anything technical in the middle of Sherwood Forest on a camping stove with one pan, cooking for Sat Bains, think again! This is a straightforward dish full of fantastic hearty flavours.

SERVES 6–8

25g lard
12 large pork sausages
4 slices of streaky bacon, chopped into 2-cm pieces
6 slices of back bacon, chopped into 2-cm pieces
1 leek, diced
1 carrot diced
2 celery sticks, diced
1 shallot, diced
sea salt and freshly ground black pepper
300g drained haricot beans (from a can or jar)
200ml cider
200ml veal jus or beef stock
1 tablespoon Worcestershire sauce
2 tablespoons runny honey
1 Bramley apple, diced
a few sprigs of rosemary
200g ham hock, shredded

To serve
a handful of carrot tops or flat-leaf parsley, chopped

Heat a large, heavy-based, non-stick sauté pan until hot. Add the lard and as soon as it has melted, add the sausages. Cook for around 5 minutes, turning regularly until golden brown. Add the bacon to the pan and fry for 2–3 minutes more.

Stir in the leek, carrot, celery and shallot, season well then add the beans and cook for another 5 minutes, stirring regularly.

Pour in the cider, the jus or stock and the Worcestershire sauce. Stir in the honey and the diced apple and add the rosemary to the pan. Increase the heat a little to bring to the boil then simmer for 5 minutes.

Add the shredded ham hock and stir to warm through. Taste to check the seasoning, sprinkle with carrot tops or parsley and serve. (Pictured overleaf.)

ROAST PORK WITH BLACK PUDDING FRITTERS & CARAMELISED APPLES

This was simply the crew's favourite dish of the whole trip. I wanted to call it 'pork and crackling and other bits' but people higher up had other ideas. Laverstoke Park Farm in Hampshire makes the best black pudding in my view, if you're searching for one.

SERVES 10–12

4kg pork loin, rind scored
sea salt and freshly ground
    black pepper
50g caster sugar
1 Bramley apple, sliced
50g walnut halves
10 cobnuts, removed from
    their shells
30g butter
300ml dry cider
300ml veal jus
200g black pudding
50g plain flour
2 eggs, beaten
50g panko breadcrumbs
1–2 litres vegetable oil,
    for deep-frying

Preheat the oven to its highest setting.

Put the pork into a big roasting tray and rub 2 tablespoons of sea salt over the rind making sure it goes into all the cuts. Roast in the oven for 30 minutes, then turn the oven down to 150°C (130°C fan)/ 300°F/gas 2 and cook for a further 3 hours.

Heat the sugar in a non-stick frying pan over a medium heat until it dissolves and caramelises. Add the apple slices and nuts, along with half of the butter and 50ml of the cider. Take the pan off the heat and set aside to cool.

To make a sauce, pour the remaining cider into a medium saucepan and add the veal jus. Bring to the boil over a medium heat and simmer until the liquid has reduced by half. Whisk in the remaining butter.

Slice the black pudding into thick rounds. Put the flour into a shallow bowl and season. Pour the eggs into a separate shallow bowl and the breadcrumbs into another. Coat each slice of black pudding in the flour, then in the beaten egg, then in the breadcrumbs.

Heat the vegetable oil in a deep-fat fryer to 180°C (350°F) or in a deep, heavy-based saucepan until a breadcrumb sizzles and turns brown when dropped into it. (Note: hot oil can be dangerous; do not leave unattended.) Line a tray with kitchen paper.

Carefully lower the coated black pudding slices into the hot oil and fry until golden and crispy. Lift out and drain on the kitchen paper. Season with salt.

To serve, place a large slice of the pork and a piece of crackling on each plate, spoon the caramelised apples and nuts alongside and add a black pudding fritter, then drizzle over the warm sauce.

NORTH YORK MOORS HEATHER LAMB

The bandstand in Whitby harbour might not be an obvious place to cook a dish
containing lamb but from here you can see the amazing moorland all around the town
that stretches for miles inland with the huge number of sheep grazing on the heather
and grassland. The heather and heather honey work so well here, coupled with
the peas from the area just beyond the Moors towards where we used to live.
Oh, and they grow great spuds in these parts too.

SERVES 4

4 x 125-g lamb loins or fillets
sea salt and freshly ground
    black pepper
1 tablespoon olive oil
1 tablespoon heather honey
small bunch of heather,
    flowers picked
25g butter

For the salad
1 large banana shallot, sliced
100g fresh peas (from approx.
    300g peas in their pods)
75g peas in their pods
2–3 asparagus spears
100g cooked new potatoes, sliced

For the dressing
50ml veal jus
25ml gin
50ml olive oil
1 teaspoon heather honey
sea salt and freshly ground
    black pepper

To serve
50g sheep's curd
elderflowers, to garnish
    (optional; when in season)

Heat a flat griddle pan over a medium heat until hot. Put the lamb
on a board and season well. Drizzle the oil over the griddle then pop
the lamb on. Drizzle the honey over the lamb, sprinkle with heather
then dot each piece with a quarter of the butter. Turn each piece of
lamb over after 2–3 minutes, coating each side in the honey butter.
Continue to cook for a further 2–3 minutes. Check the centre of each
piece of lamb has reached 70°C (160°F) using a cook's thermometer,
then lift onto a board, cover and leave to rest.

To make the salad, pop the sliced shallot and both types of peas
into a large salad bowl. Snap the woody ends off the asparagus spears
and discard, then use a potato peeler to slice the spears into ribbons.
Add these to the bowl, together with the potatoes, and toss
everything together.

Whisk all the ingredients for the dressing in a separate bowl
and season well. Spoon over the salad and toss together.

To serve, pile the salad onto a platter. Slice the lamb into 2-cm
pieces and arrange on top. Dot the curd cheese all over and scatter
with the elderflowers, if using. (Pictured overleaf.)

BBQ LAMB CHOPS WITH CHIMICHURRI SAUCE, BROCCOLINI & NEW POTATOES

This dish is simply lamb and mint sauce. Chimichurri is a green sauce that originates from Argentina and Uruguay and is usually made with parsley, garlic, olive oil and red wine vinegar. Adding mint to it makes it a great, simple fresh-tasting sauce that goes beautifully with barbecued or grilled lamb chops.

SERVES 4

400g new potatoes
25ml olive oil
8 lamb chops
sea salt and freshly ground
    black pepper
200g broccolini

For the chimichurri sauce
15g flat-leaf parsley,
    roughly chopped
15g coriander,
    roughly chopped
15g mint, leaves picked
    and roughly chopped
2 garlic cloves, chopped
1 green chilli, chopped
1 shallot, chopped
25ml red wine vinegar
50ml olive oil

Light your BBQ. When the coals are silvery in colour, it's ready to cook on.

While you're waiting for the coals to heat, bring a large pan of salted water to the boil and cook the new potatoes for 10 minutes until just tender.

When the BBQ is ready, rub a little oil over the lamb chops and season well. Put the potatoes and broccolini into a bowl and add the remaining oil. Season and toss together.

Put the chops onto the BBQ and cook for 3–4 minutes on each side. Add the potatoes and broccolini when you turn the chops over and turn these over after 1–2 minutes.

To make the sauce, mix all the ingredients together in a bowl and season well.

To serve, pile the lamb, potatoes and broccolini onto a platter and spoon over the sauce.

WELSH LAMB WITH GNOCCHI & VEGETABLES

To top off the trip through Wales, I had the best meal I've ever eaten in Britain at Ynyshir near Machynlleth. Both Stephen Terry and I had wanted to go and taste the food by Gareth Ward and it didn't disappoint, from the moment we walked in with The Rolling Stones on vinyl playing in the restaurant to the last of the 20 courses we had here. It's brilliant cooking and if you want my tip of where to go to eat, you have to put this place on your list. Oh, and the lamb is great too.

SERVES 4

12 small lamb chops
200g Welsh sheep's curd cheese
sea salt and freshly ground
  black pepper
25ml olive oil
500g cooked potato,
  pushed through a ricer
125g plain flour
2 egg yolks
4 heritage carrots,
  halved lengthways
1 large leek, sliced
8 spears asparagus, trimmed
½ spring cabbage, tough stems
  removed and leaves torn
50g butter
zest and juice of 1 lemon
small bunch of mint, leaves
  picked and chopped

Preheat a large, flat griddle pan over a medium heat until hot.

Using a sharp knife, cut a pocket through the fat side of the lamb, right into the meaty part. Set aside half of the cheese, then fill each pocket with around a teaspoonful of the rest. Season the lamb all over then drizzle the oil over the hot griddle pan and pop the lamb on to cook for 2–3 minutes on each side. It should be golden on the outside and feel slightly firm when pressed. Transfer to a plate, cover and leave to rest. Turn off the heat under the griddle but leave it on the hob for later to cook the vegetables.

To make the gnocchi, mix the potato, flour, egg yolks, the remaining cheese and some seasoning together in a bowl until well combined and smooth. Divide into 4 portions then roll each one into a long thin sausage (about 20cm long and 2cm thick), using a little extra flour. Cut each sausage into 3-cm pieces.

Bring a large pan of salted water to the boil and cook the gnocchi in batches for 2 minutes, then use a slotted spoon to lift out and set aside on a plate.

Bring a separate large pan of salted water to the boil and blanch the carrots, leek and asparagus for 2–3 minutes. Reheat the griddle pan over a medium heat until hot. Drain the vegetables well, then put onto the hot griddle with the cabbage and cook for 3–4 minutes, coating it all with the lamb fat. Spoon onto a plate.

Add the butter, lemon zest and juice, the mint and 50ml water to the griddle pan and stir to make a sauce. Mix all the vegetables and gnocchi together back on the griddle plate, then season and spoon onto 4 warm plates. Top with the lamb chops, drizzle over the sauce and serve.

TAGINE OF LAMB CHOPS

Wapping Wharf is a testament to what's happening in Bristol right now with new buildings and flats popping up all around and along the old docks. It's still in its infancy but there are a few restaurants, one of which was a highlight for me – the small and compact BOX-E run by husband and wife Elliott and Tessa Lidstone – as were the two food containers there, one selling cheese and the other some great local meats. You'll find great lamb all around the West Country from local suppliers.

SERVES 2

1 tablespoon olive oil
sea salt and freshly ground
    black pepper
2 x 200-g Barnsley lamb chops
½ onion, diced
2 garlic cloves, chopped
6 medium tomatoes, quartered
50ml Harveys Bristol cream
    sherry
½ teaspoon ground coriander
½ teaspoon ground cumin
½ teaspoon chilli flakes
½ teaspoon ground cinnamon
½ teaspoon paprika
¼ teaspoon ground nutmeg
5-cm piece fresh ginger, grated
2-cm piece fresh turmeric, grated
1 tablespoon runny honey
25g flaked almonds
small bunch of fresh coriander,
    chopped

Heat a large, non-stick frying pan over a medium heat then pour in the oil. Season the chops all over then pop them into the pan and cook for 2–3 minutes until well browned. Flip them over and continue to cook for a further 2–3 minutes.

Add the diced onion, garlic and tomatoes, then pour in the sherry. Use a wooden spoon to stir any juices in the base of the pan into the ingredients.

Add all of the dry spices, stir again, then add the grated ginger and turmeric. Stir and season well. Keep the pan over a medium heat and cook for 5 minutes – it should be gently bubbling.

Check the seasoning then divide between 2 warmed bowls, drizzle with the honey and sprinkle over the almonds and coriander.

LAMB HOT POT

This is a classic British dish that had to be in a book like this. Don't leave out the kidneys and the Worcestershire sauce, though. They're essential for a great flavour.

SERVES 6

2 tablespoons vegetable oil
1kg diced lamb leg
1kg diced lamb shoulder
sea salt and freshly ground
 black pepper
3 large onions, sliced
6 lamb's kidneys, cleaned
 and chopped
500ml lamb stock
1 tablespoon Worcestershire
 sauce
a few sprigs of rosemary
1kg Maris Piper potatoes,
 sliced
65g butter
6 large leeks, sliced

Heat the oil in a 4-litre casserole pan over a medium heat and fry the lamb leg and shoulder, in batches, until browned all over. Season each batch as you cook it and set aside on a plate once cooked until all the lamb is done.

Add the onions to the same pan, season again and cook, stirring every now and then, for 5 minutes until starting to soften. Pop the lamb back into the pan and add the kidneys. Pour in the stock and add the Worcestershire sauce and sprigs of rosemary. Season well and stir together.

Cover the pan with a lid, bring to the boil then turn the heat down and simmer on a low heat, very gently, for 2 hours until the lamb is tender. Have a look after 1½ hours and add a splash of water if it's looking dry. To check the meat is cooked, pull a piece apart with 2 forks – it should shred easily.

Preheat the oven to 180°C (160°C fan)/350°F/gas 4. Uncover the pan and arrange the sliced potatoes all over the top to cover the meat. Dot with 15g of the butter, then season and cook in the oven for 45 minutes.

When the hot pot is almost ready, pop the leeks into a pan with the remaining butter and 100ml water. Season well and cook over a medium heat for 3–4 minutes until the leeks are cooked through and tender. Serve alongside the hot pot.

CHEESY POTATO & LAMB PIE

The crew made me cook this as they wanted it, and by the look of what little was left I think they liked it! I cooked it again for the show and the same thing happened. Dishes like this make me smile as they are as much about the food as they are about the story of how they came about, so thank Matt the sound man as it was his idea.

SERVES 6–8

1 kg floury potatoes, such as King Edward or Maris Piper
75g butter
1 onion, finely sliced
700g lamb mince
sea salt and freshly ground black pepper
2 tablespoons Worcestershire sauce
500ml beef stock
1 large bunch of flat-leaf parsley, chopped
100ml double cream

For the rarebit
400g cheddar cheese, grated
50ml Welsh bitter
a few drops of Tabasco sauce
1 tablespoon Worcestershire sauce
1 tablespoon English mustard
1 tablespoon plain flour
2 egg yolks

To serve
450g frozen peas

Peel the potatoes and chop into evenly sized chunks. Put them in a large pan, cover with cold water, pop the lid on and bring to a simmer. Cook for around 15–20 minutes until tender. Drain well in a colander, then pass them through a ricer and set aside.

Heat a large, non-stick frying pan over a medium heat until hot. Add 25g of the butter, stir in the onion and fry for 5–8 minutes. Add the lamb mince to the pan and season well. Cook over a high heat until browned all over, stirring well to break up the pieces, then stir in the Worcestershire sauce and beef stock. Bring to a simmer and cook over a medium heat for 20 minutes. Stir in the parsley and season well.

For the rarebit, tip the cheese into a large pan. Pour in the beer, followed by the Tabasco, Worcestershire sauce and mustard. Place over a low heat and cook until the cheese has melted.

Line a tray with baking parchment. When all the cheese has melted, stir in the flour and cook gently for a minute or two. Season and add the egg yolks and beat together. Pour onto the lined tray and spread out to a rectangle roughly 30 x 20cm and leave to cool.

For the potatoes, melt the remaining butter in a large pan over a medium heat then pour in the cream and heat for a minute. Season well then spoon in the potatoes and mash together. Keep the pan on the hob until it's warmed through, stirring occasionally.

Preheat the grill until hot. Spoon the lamb into a 30 x 20cm, deep ovenproof dish, then spread the mash over the top to cover the meat. Invert the cooled rarebit on top of the mash and peel off the baking paper. Sit the dish on a lipped baking tray and slide under the grill for 5 minutes, until the rarebit is golden and bubbling.

While the dish is under the grill, cook the peas following the timings on the bag. Drain well and serve with the pie.

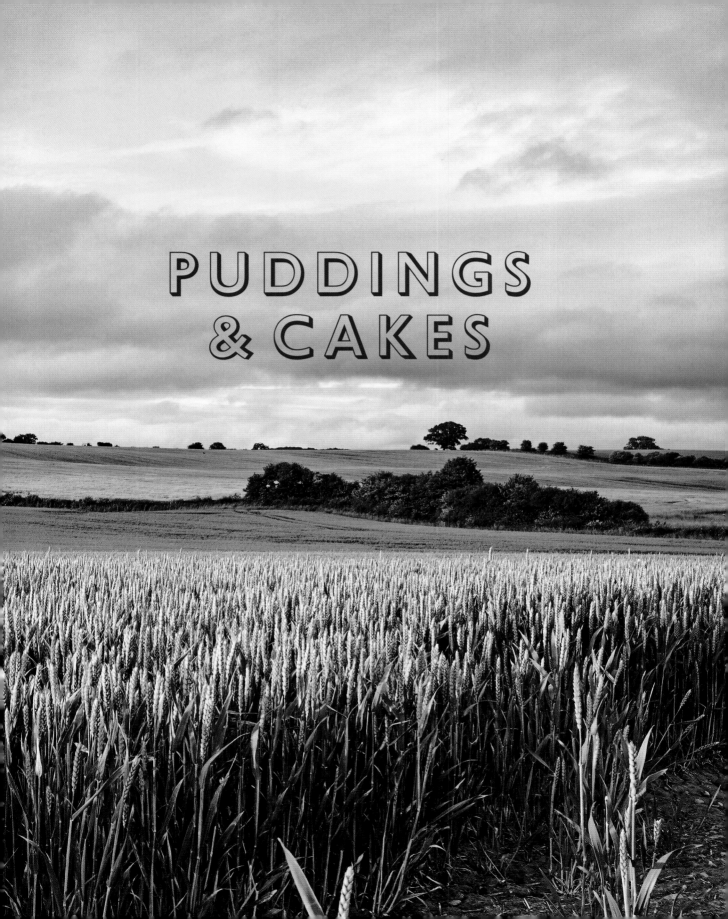

PUDDINGS & CAKES

BRANDY SNAPS WITH SCOTCH WHISKY CREAM

The Hull Fair takes place every October and is Europe's largest travelling fair and one of the oldest, dating back to 1278. No visit to the fair is complete without a bag of brandy snaps from Wright & Co of Brighouse. The 'brandy snap' name comes from the spirit you can add to the cream but here I've added whisky instead (from the fellow at Edradour Distillery, pictured on page 213). You can fill them with whatever you wish; either way, making brandy snaps at home and filling them is just a joy to do.

MAKES 18

100g butter
100g light soft brown sugar
100g golden syrup
100g plain flour
1 teaspoon ground ginger
25g rolled oats

For the filling
1 litre double cream
75ml Scotch whisky

Line 2 baking sheets with baking parchment.

Heat the butter, sugar and syrup together in a medium pan over a low to medium heat, stirring all the time.

Tip the flour and ground ginger into a bowl. Pour the syrup mixture into the bowl and beat all the ingredients together until smooth. Cover with clingfilm and chill in the fridge for 1 hour.

Preheat the oven to 170°C (150°C fan)/340°F/gas 3.

Divide the mixture roughly into 18 portions and roll each one into a ball. Place 3 on each baking sheet, leaving plenty of space between the balls as they'll spread as they bake. Place the baking sheets in the oven for 3–4 minutes, then take them out and sprinkle with oats before returning to the oven for another 3 minutes.

Allow to cool slightly, then use a palette knife to lift up one of the discs and wrap it around a large wooden spoon handle to form a rolled brandy snap. Place on a wire rack to cool and set hard. Continue until you've rolled all the discs – you'll need to work quickly while they're still warm. If they've cooled down and are too hard to roll, return to the oven for 30 seconds so they're malleable enough to shape.

Bake and roll the remaining brandy snaps in 2 more batches of 6 until you have a total of 18.

Whip the cream in a bowl until just starting to hold its shape. Whisk in the whisky, then spoon into a piping bag. Pipe the cream into either end of the brandy snaps and serve straightaway.

RASPBERRY SUMMER PUDDING WITH WHISKY CREAM

Scotland is famous for its delicious raspberries and what better to serve with this raspberry pudding than whisky cream. I made this perched on a grassy knoll in the centre of Edinburgh on a Friday evening as the pubs were getting busy, wearing a kilt! I'd never worn one before – if you want to experience the full Scottish dress, go to Kinloch Anderson. They've been making kilts here in the family business for over 100 years and you really need to see the sheer skill and work that goes into making them. It's really impressive, as is the weight of the finished outfit.

SERVES 4

1 teaspoon vegetable oil
1kg raspberries
8 thin slices of white bread

To serve
300ml double cream
25ml whisky cream liqueur
a few sprigs of mint
12 large raspberries

Lightly grease a 1-litre pudding basin with the oil and line it with clingfilm, leaving extra hanging over the edge (to wrap over later).

Put 400g of the raspberries in a food processor and whizz until smooth to make a sauce.

Cut a slice of bread into a circle to fit the base of the pudding basin and another to fit the top of the bowl. With the remaining slices of bread, chop off the crusts and discard (or whizz them into breadcrumbs in a food processor and freeze for future use), then cut each slice of bread in half to make 12 rectangles.

Pour the raspberry sauce into a shallow bowl and dip the small circle into the sauce, coating it on both sides. Place into the bottom of the lined basin. Next, dip a rectangle into the raspberry sauce and place up the side. Repeat, using all the rectangles to line the bowl, making sure they overlap slightly.

Spoon half of the remaining sauce over the remaining raspberries and toss to coat, then spoon these into the lined bowl and push down with the back of a spoon to pack them in tightly. Dip the large circle of bread in the remaining raspberry sauce, again turning it over so it's completely coated, and place on top.

Bring the clingfilm up and over the top of the pudding to cover and press down tightly. Chill for at least 1 hour or up to 8 hours.

When you're ready to serve, pull the clingfilm back, then upturn the bowl onto a serving plate. Lift the bowl away, then peel off the clingfilm. Spoon any remaining raspberry sauce all over the pudding to cover up any white patches.

Whip the cream in a bowl until the mixture stands in soft peaks then pour the whisky cream liqueur over the top and fold in.

Decorate the pudding with the mint and raspberries on the top and around the sides and serve with the whisky cream.

RASPBERRY MOUSSE
WITH MACAROONS

This mousse topped with beautiful macaroons is perfect for a special occasion. We grabbed our macaroons from Miss Macaroon in Birmingham but don't worry, she (aka Rosie Ginday, ex-team member of Glynn Purnell's Michelin-starred restaurant) has an online shop. It's the only macaroon shop in the world where your macaroons can be Pantone-matched to any colour you wish.

SERVES 10

600g full-fat cream cheese
500ml double cream
juice of 1 lemon
300ml full-fat crème fraîche
400g raspberries
36 x 4-cm shop-bought
   macaroons

In a large bowl, whisk together the cream cheese and double cream until the cream is mixed in. Add the lemon juice, then the crème fraîche, and continue to whisk the mixture just until it thickens.

Add the raspberries and gently stir them in so they create a ripple effect through the mixture.

Place a 24-cm metal ring on a cake stand and spoon the mixture into the ring. Use a palette knife to level off the top so it's smooth and chill in the fridge for up to 1 hour.

Use a blow torch on a medium heat to quickly heat the outside of the ring and loosen the mousse (or slip a hot palette knife around the edge) then carefully lift off the ring. Arrange the macaroons evenly over the mousse to cover the top.

Slice into portions to serve.

BLACKBERRY MOUSSE WITH SALTED CARAMEL CHOCOLATE POPCORN

This dish is totally bonkers, I know, but I had a Willy Wonka moment. If you want a fun piece for the table at the end of a dinner, this is perfect and it's great fun to eat.

SERVES 10

6 gelatine leaves
400ml ready-made
   fresh custard
500g blackberries
600ml double cream
3 egg whites
3 tablespoons caster sugar

For the popcorn
200g dark chocolate,
   broken into pieces
1 tablespoon vegetable oil
100g popcorn kernels
100ml dulce de leche
1 teaspoon sea salt flakes

Put the gelatine leaves in a bowl of cold water and leave to soak for 2–3 minutes. Pour the custard into a medium saucepan and warm through gently.

Whizz the blackberries in a food processor to make a smooth purée. Turn off the heat under the custard, then stir half the blackberry purée into it. Lift the gelatine out of the water and squeeze out any excess, then stir into the custard and mix together thoroughly. Pour into a large bowl, add the rest of the blackberry purée and stir again to thoroughly combine.

Whip the cream in a separate bowl until thick and soft peaks form.

Wash the whisks well and in a separate, clean, grease-free bowl, whisk the egg whites to stiff peaks, then whisk in all the sugar.

Add a spoonful of the meringue to the blackberry mixture and fold in using a large metal spoon. Once smooth, fold in the remainder of the meringue and all the whipped cream. Fold everything together until the mousse is well combined, then pour into a large serving bowl and transfer to the fridge to set for at least 4 hours or overnight.

When you're ready to serve, make the popcorn. Melt the chocolate in a bowl resting over a pan of hot water (make sure the base doesn't touch the water).

Heat a large, non-stick saucepan with a lid and add the oil and popcorn. Put the lid on and wait for the popcorn to pop, shaking the pan occasionally.

Add the dulce de leche to the melted chocolate and stir together until smooth. Pour the mixture over the popcorn and mix thoroughly. Add the salt and mix again.

Pile the coated popcorn on top of the mousse and sprinkle with more salt (if you wish) before serving straightaway.

GOLDEN SYRUP STEAMED PUDDING WITH RHUBARB & CUSTARD

This classic pudding had to be in a book like this but the addition of the rhubarb cuts through the sweetness and adds a nice twist. The best rhubarb is grown in the rhubarb triangle, an area between Wakefield, Morley and Rothwell in Yorkshire, which has the perfect environment and soil. The area used to be over twice the size but it still produces nearly 90 per cent of the world's winter forced rhubarb.

SERVES 6

200g butter, softened,
   plus extra for greasing
3 tablespoons golden syrup
200g caster sugar
2 vanilla pods, halved
   lengthways
3 eggs, beaten
200g self-raising flour

For the rhubarb
400g rhubarb, chopped
   into 2.5-cm pieces
100g caster sugar
zest and juice of 2 oranges

For the custard
8 egg yolks
80g caster sugar
300ml double cream
300ml milk

Lightly butter a 1.2-litre heatproof pudding basin and spoon the golden syrup into the bottom.

Put the butter and sugar into a large mixing bowl and beat well with an electric hand whisk until light and fluffy. Scrape the seeds from the vanilla pods into the bowl and stir in. Put the pods aside for the custard.

Add the eggs one at a time, beating well after each addition, then add the flour and fold in using a large metal spoon to make a smooth, thick batter.

Spoon the batter into the pudding basin. Cut a piece of greaseproof paper several centimetres wider than the rim of the basin. Do the same with a piece of foil and put it on top of the paper. Holding the paper and foil together, fold a pleat down the middle (this allows it to expand as the pudding steams) and place over the bowl, smooth it over the rim and tie with string to secure it. Fold a large piece of foil into a long strip and place under the pudding bowl to use as a handle later.

Place a saucer upside down in the bottom of a large saucepan. Lift the basin onto the saucer with the foil strip underneath and folded on top so you can lift the bowl out later. Pour boiling water into the pan to come two-thirds of the way up the bowl then cover with a lid and bring to the boil. Reduce the heat and simmer for 1–1½ hours until a skewer inserted into the centre of the pudding comes out clean. Keep an eye on the water level while the pudding is cooking – add hot water from the kettle if it's getting low.

Heat the rhubarb, sugar, orange zest and juice and 75ml water in a saucepan over a low heat. Cover with a lid and simmer gently for 10–15 minutes, until the rhubarb is tender but still holds its shape.

To make the custard, whisk the egg yolks and sugar together in a bowl. Pour the cream and milk into a pan over a medium heat, add the reserved vanilla pods and bring to the boil. As soon as it comes to the boil, pour it into the egg mixture and stir thoroughly to mix together. Remove the vanilla pods and pour it back into the pan and stir constantly over a gentle heat until thickened, taking care not to overcook or you'll end up with scrambled eggs!

Lift the pudding out of the pan and leave to cool for 5 minutes. Take the foil and greaseproof paper off the basin then upturn the pudding onto a large plate. Serve with the custard and the poached rhubarb alongside.

BREAD & BUTTER PUDDING WITH CHERRY COMPOTE

The keys to a great bread and butter pudding have to be the egg and egg yolk combo, the cooking time and temperature of the oven. Too many eggs and it tastes eggy, too hot an oven and the mix will soufflé and split, too long in the oven and it will be too firm. When made right, it's a great dessert and one that should be on menus around the country. By the way, Paul Ainsworth doesn't make a bad one at Number 6 in Padstow.

SERVES 6–8

100g butter, at room temperature
1 loaf medium-sliced white bread
4 eggs
8 egg yolks
200g caster sugar
1 teaspoon vanilla bean paste
300ml milk
300ml double cream
2 tablespoons icing sugar

For the compote
200g cherries, pitted
50g caster sugar

Preheat the oven to 150°C (130°C fan)/300°F/gas 2.

Butter each slice of bread on one side only, then cut off the crusts. Slice each piece in half diagonally to make 2 triangles. Lay them in a 30 x 20cm ovenproof dish, overlapping each slice as you go.

To make the custard, put the eggs and egg yolks into a large bowl and add the sugar and vanilla bean paste. Whisk together to break down the eggs then pour in the milk and cream and continue to whisk until smooth. Pour as much of the mixture over the bread as possible to cover and set aside to soak for about 20 minutes – you won't use all the custard at this stage. Keep topping up with more custard until all of it has been poured into the dish.

Transfer to the oven and bake for 35–40 minutes. The pudding should be bubbling hot but not necessarily golden brown.

To make the compote, put the cherries and sugar into a saucepan. Heat gently to dissolve the sugar then bring to the boil and simmer for 10 minutes. Allow to cool slightly and pour into a bowl.

Dust the bread and butter pudding with the icing sugar and use a blow torch to caramelise the sugar or place it under a hot grill for a couple of minutes.

Spoon into bowls and serve with the compote alongside.

SHERWOOD FOREST PEARS WITH WALNUTS, STILTON & OAT PANCAKES

North Staffordshire and Stoke-on-Trent are the main homes of oatcakes. Derbyshire has its version, too, and I've also seen Pennine oatcakes on my travels but these are usually made with buttermilk. Whichever type you make, they will all work with simple poached pears and blue cheese. I love them in this salad with honeycomb and walnuts. It makes a great end to a meal (or even a starter).

SERVES 4

6 small pears, peeled,
  halved and cored
100g caster sugar
4 fresh elderflower heads
  (optional, when in season) or
  1 tablespoon elderflower cordial

For the pancakes
125g medium oatmeal
125g wholemeal flour
1 teaspoon sea salt
1 teaspoon caster sugar
500ml full-fat milk
1 tablespoon vegetable oil

For the candied walnuts
200g walnut halves
100g caster sugar

To serve
8 celery hearts and leaves
4 fresh elderflower heads
  (optional, when in season)
200g blue Stilton, crumbled
25g honeycomb

Start by making the pancake batter so it has a chance to rest. Whisk the oatmeal, flour, salt, sugar and milk together in a bowl until smooth. Cover and leave to rest for 1 hour.

Put the pears, sugar and fresh elderflowers or cordial into a pan and pour in enough water to cover. Pop a lid on and bring to the boil then simmer for 10 minutes. Drain well and set aside.

To make the candied walnuts, put the walnuts and sugar into a medium saucepan with 1 tablespoon water and heat gently to dissolve the sugar. Turn the heat up slightly to caramelise the sugar and stir constantly to coat the nuts until they are candied. Tip onto a plate lined with baking parchment or silicone to cool.

Heat a large, flat griddle pan (or use a large, heavy-based frying pan) over a medium heat until hot, drizzle with oil and spoon about a dessertspoonful of the pancake mixture into the pan. Fit as many pancakes as you can in the pan, and cook for 1 minute until golden. Flip over and cook for a further minute on the other side until light golden. Continue cooking the pancakes until all the batter has been used up.

Put the celery hearts and leaves and elderflowers (if using) into a bowl of iced water to crisp them up.

To serve, pop the pancakes onto a platter, top with the pears, crumbled Stilton and celery. Scatter over the walnuts, dot with pieces of the honeycomb and finish with the elderflowers.

DAMSON UPSIDE-DOWN CAKE WITH CIDER CUSTARD

'Plant a plum for your son but plant a damson for your grandson' – that's how long these trees take to bear fruit. I should know – I'm still waiting for a crop from the trees in my garden. If you're lucky enough to have damsons, this is the perfect cake to make but you can use regular plums instead.

SERVES 8

200g butter, softened
200g caster sugar
4 eggs
200g self-raising flour
1 apple, cored and sliced
200g damsons, halved
   and stoned

For the custard
8 egg yolks
75g caster sugar
100ml cider
300ml double cream

Preheat the oven to 180°C (160°C fan)/350°F/gas 4. Grease a 23-cm round cake tin and line with baking parchment.

Put the butter and sugar into the bowl of a freestanding mixer fitted with a K-beater. Beat together on a medium speed until the sugar has mixed into the butter and the mixture looks pale and almost white. Beat in the eggs, one at a time, adding a little flour if the mixture looks as though it might curdle, then take the bowl out of the stand. Use a large metal spoon to fold in the flour, along with half of the apple.

Arrange the remaining apple in the bottom of the tin, spaced apart, then scatter over the damsons evenly. Spoon the cake batter on top, spreading it out so it covers the fruit and is even, then bake in the oven for 40 minutes or until golden and a skewer inserted into the centre comes out clean.

Make the custard. Whisk the egg yolks and sugar together in a bowl until just combined. Pour the cider and cream into a medium pan and heat gently until warm, then pour over the eggs and sugar and whisk everything together. Pour the custard back into the pan and heat gently, continuing to whisk until it starts to thicken. It's ready when it coats the back of a spoon. Strain through a sieve resting over a bowl, then pour into a jug.

Upturn the cake onto a plate and peel off the baking paper. Slice and serve with the custard poured over the top.

WELSH CAKES WITH BERRIES & HONEY

Welsh cakes, or bakestones, are simple to make and taste so much better to me if they're made by rubbing the ingredients by hand. Cooked on a flat griddle pan with no fat, they can be eaten hot or cold but I think they're best at room temperature. There are different variations, including Welsh dragons, which have grated apple added; jam splits, which are popular in South Wales; and in the Welsh mountains they add baking powder to make them rise more.

MAKES 16

350g self-raising flour,
    plus extra for dusting
2 teaspoons baking powder
1 teaspoon mixed spice
100g currants
115g caster sugar,
    plus extra to serve
175g butter, diced and chilled
1 egg, beaten
2 tablespoons full-fat milk

To serve
400g raspberries
    and strawberries
runny honey

Heat a flat griddle pan over a medium heat until hot.

In a bowl, mix together the flour, baking powder, spice, currants and caster sugar.

Add the butter and rub into the dry ingredients using your fingertips until the mixture resembles fine crumbs. Pour in the egg and milk and mix with a spoon or table knife to form a soft dough. Shape into a round disc and flatten slightly.

Lightly flour a clean work surface and a rolling pin and roll out until the dough is around 1cm thick. Use a 7-cm round cutter and stamp out 16 rounds, re-rolling the dough as necessary.

Pop the cakes onto the hot griddle and cook in batches for 3 minutes on each side. Take them off the pan, set aside on a large plate and sprinkle with extra caster sugar.

To serve, pile up the Welsh cakes, top with the berries, drizzle with a little honey and serve.

BLACKBURN & ECCLES CAKES

A combination of Blackburn cakes, which contain cooked apple, and the classic Eccles cakes, which are filled with currants, these delicious pastry cakes are a must on a cheese board. Other similar cakes from around the country are Chorley cakes, which are less sweet with a shortcrust pastry and Banbury cakes, which are a larger oval version of a classic Eccles.

MAKES 12

450g strong white bread flour, plus extra for dusting
250g cold butter, grated
a pinch of salt
200ml iced water
1 egg white
25g caster sugar

For the filling
1 large Bramley apple (around 360g), diced
35g salted butter
100g currants
25g caster sugar
25g light soft brown sugar

To serve
Stilton and cheddar cheese

First make the filling. Put the diced apple into a small pan with ½ tablespoon water, cover with a lid, and cook gently over a low heat until they start to break down. Spoon into a shallow bowl, spread out thinly (so it cools quicker) and chill.

Melt the butter in a separate pan and add the currants and both types of sugar. Stir together and cook over a low heat for 2 minutes. Spoon into a bowl and chill.

Now make the pastry. Tip the flour into a bowl and stir in the butter and salt. Drizzle the water over the top and mix with a round-bladed table knife to bring the mixture together to make a rough dough. Use your hands to gently and quickly knead the mixture until smooth. Form the pastry into a disc, wrap in clingfilm and chill for 30 minutes.

Preheat the oven to 200°C (180°C fan)/400°F/gas 6.

Dust a clean work surface with flour. Divide the dough into 4 even pieces. Roll out one piece until it's around 3–4mm thick. Use a 10-cm round cutter to stamp out 3 rounds. Divide the apple mixture roughly into 12 and put a spoonful into the middle of each round of pastry. Do the same with the currant mixture. Fold the pastry over the filling and seal together tightly. Flip over, shape into a round, and pop onto a large baking sheet. Do the same with the rest of the pastry and filling until you've shaped 12 cakes.

Brush each pastry cake with egg white and sprinkle with a little caster sugar, then cut 2 or 3 slits in the top of each with a knife. Bake for 30–35 minutes, until golden and the pastry is crisp.

Cool on a wire rack until warm and serve with the cheese.

CHOCOLATE STOUT CAKE

Stout is a dark, rich top-fermented beer and is the only type of beer you can use for this cake and the icing, so don't start going off-piste and using Stella or other stuff – it won't work!

SERVES 10

200g butter
150g dark chocolate, broken into pieces
300ml stout
4 eggs
500g soft light brown sugar
350g self-raising flour

For the icing
400g full-fat cream cheese
25ml stout
200g icing sugar
a couple of squares of dark or milk chocolate, to decorate

Preheat the oven to 160°C (140°C fan)/320°F/gas 3. Line a 27-cm, deep-sided cake tin with greaseproof paper.

Put the butter, chocolate and stout into a large heatproof bowl and rest over a pan of just-simmering water, making sure the base doesn't touch the water, until the butter and chocolate have melted. Lift the bowl off the pan and leave to cool slightly.

Add the eggs and sugar to the mixture and whisk well, then fold in the flour until the mixture is smooth.

Pour the cake batter into the prepared tin and bake for 1 hour. Leave to cool in the tin before turning out.

To make the icing, whisk the cream cheese, stout and icing sugar together in a bowl until smooth. Spoon on top of the cake and spread out to cover. Grate the chocolate over the top and serve.

CHOCOLATE & CHERRY GIN CAKE

Cherries, chocolate and kirsch are, of course, the classic ingredients of Black Forest gâteau, a staple cake in British homes and on menus in the 1970s and '80s. This cake is a more up-to-date version using gin. The number of different varieties of gin being produced now around the country is crazy but my favourite from my travels is Forager's Gin from the Snowdonia Distillery in Wales. It's as delicious with tonic and ice as it is with this cake. They only make small batches of the stuff but get hold of it if you can and tell me what you think.

MAKES 2 CAKES, EACH SERVES 8

9 eggs
250g caster sugar
1 teaspoon vanilla bean paste
40g cocoa powder,
  plus extra to decorate
200g self-raising flour

For the syrup
100ml gin
100g caster sugar
300g cherries with stalks

For the jam
300g pitted cherries
50g caster sugar

For the cream
750ml double cream
50ml gin

Line 2 x 20-cm deep-sided cake tins with greaseproof paper. Preheat the oven to 180°C (160°C fan)/350°F/gas 4.

To make the syrup, pour the gin and sugar into a saucepan. Heat to dissolve the sugar, then add the cherries and set aside to cool.

Next make the jam. Put the cherries and sugar into a heavy-based medium pan and heat gently to dissolve the sugar. Bring to a simmer and cook for 2–3 minutes until the fruit has cooked down and is jammy.

To make the cakes, whisk the eggs and sugar together in the bowl of a freestanding mixer until thick and mousse-like. This takes around 10 minutes. Whisk in the vanilla then add the cocoa and flour and fold in using a large metal spoon until everything is combined, making sure there are no floury bits left.

Divide the cake batter evenly between the lined tins and bake for 25–30 minutes or until a skewer (or cocktail stick) inserted into the centre comes out clean. Cool in the tins for 5 minutes, then turn each cake out to cool completely. Wrap one in clingfilm and freeze for up to a month (see below). Remove the paper from the other cake.

Whip the cream and gin together in a bowl until the mixture forms soft peaks. Spoon into a piping bag, fitted with a 1-cm nozzle.

Place the cake on a board and use a serrated bread knife to carefully slice horizontally into three layers. Spoon some of the syrup over each layer. Put the bottom layer onto a serving plate, pipe cream all over and spread with jam. Lift the middle layer on top and do the same with the cream and jam. Finally, place the top layer on and pipe rosettes of cream all over (if you like). Dust with cocoa powder and top with the gin syrup-poached cherries.

JAMES'S TIP
This cake freezes beautifully and will still have a lovely light texture once thawed. Take out of the freezer the night before you want to use it and thaw at cool room temperature, then unwrap and fill, as above.

LARDY CAKE

Originally from the West Country, the lardy cake is the classic English tea bread. Some claim the cake came from Hampshire and Essex, others from Kent and the list goes on and on. Even Yorkshire can be in contention with its dripping cake. Either way, it graces menus everywhere from royal dinners to Gran's suppers, so it rightly deserved a place on the show and in this book.

SERVES 8

450g strong white bread flour, plus extra for kneading
150g lard, cubed
50g caster sugar
1 teaspoon salt
225g mixed dried fruit
10g fresh yeast
300ml lukewarm water

For the glaze
250g caster sugar

To serve
clotted cream
raspberry jam

Grease and line a 23-cm round cake tin with baking parchment.

Tip the flour into the bowl of a freestanding mixer fitted with a dough hook. Add the lard and sugar and mix for 1 minute until combined, then add the salt and dried fruit.

Put the yeast and water into a jug and mix together until the yeast has dissolved, then pour this into the flour mixture and mix to form a soft, sticky dough. Lightly flour a clean work surface, tip out the dough and knead for 3 minutes until smooth.

Shape the dough into a round and lift into the prepared cake tin. Cover with a clean tea towel and leave to prove for 1 hour until the dough has roughly doubled in size.

Preheat oven to 190°C (170°C fan)/370°F/gas 5. When it's proved, bake the lardy cake for 45 minutes until golden, then turn out onto a cooling rack set over a baking tray.

To make the glaze, pour 100ml water into a saucepan and add the sugar. Heat gently to dissolve the sugar and make a thick sugar syrup. Brush the syrup all over the top of the lardy cake, letting it drip onto the baking tray below.

Slice and serve with clotted cream and raspberry jam.

INDEX

WITH THANKS

To all the brilliant chefs and food people involved in the TV show:

Nick Nairn – chef, consultant and food campaigner, runs two Cook Schools at Port of Menteith and Aberdeen.

Paul Rankin – chef and author.

Tom Kitchin – chef and owner of Michelin-starred restaurant The Kitchin in Edinburgh.

Lisa Goodwin-Allen – Executive Chef of Northcote, the Michelin-starred restaurant in Blackburn, Lancashire

Michel Roux Snr – legendary chef, restaurateur, author, teacher... Works alongside his son at three-Michelin-starred The Waterside Inn, Bray.

Alain Roux – son of Michel, chef-patron of The Waterside Inn.

Paul Ainsworth – chef-patron of Michelin-starred Paul Ainsworth at No.6 in Padstow, Cornwall.

Stephen Terry – head chef of The Hardwick Restaurant in Abergavenny, Wales.

Michael Caines – chef-patron of Michelin-starred Lympstone Manor, Devon.

Mark Sargeant – chef and restaurateur, Rocksalt in Folkestone, Kent.

Sat Bains – chef-proprietor of Michelin-starred Restaurant Sat Bains in Nottingham.

Galton Blackiston – owner and chef-patron of Michelin-starred Morston Hall in Norfolk.

Grace Dent – TV food critic and restaurant critic for the Guardian.

Romy Gill – owner and head chef at Romy's Kitchen restaurant in Thornbury, Gloucestershire.

Lenny Carr-Roberts – chef-patron of The Fox, Crawley, Hampshire.

Gareth Ward – chef-patron of Michelin-starred Ynyshir, Wales.

To the film crew and all at Blue Marlin Television: Ash, Jonny and Mad Dog on camera; sound man Matt; producers Bridget and Hannah; and Dino the director.

To the home economist crew – Sam Head and Victoria Copley.

To Clare Ely and Jane Beacon at ITV for looking ahead and helping us make a great show. I hope you like the end result.

To the book team at Quadrille, and Peter Cassidy for his photography.